Beyond the Gods

Beyond the Gods

Taoist and Buddhist Mysticism

JOHN BLOFELD

London   George Allen & Unwin Ltd
Ruskin House   Museum Street

First published in 1974

ISBN 0 04 294084 2 hardback
ISBN 0 04 294085 0 paperback

Printed in Great Britain
in 11 point Plantin type
by Clarke, Doble & Brendon Ltd
Plymouth

Dedication

To James, my son, and to all who
are moved by divine discontent

Acknowledgements

I am deeply grateful to the Columbia Press and to Dr Burton Watson for consenting to my quoting several passages from Dr Watson's delightful translation, *The Complete Works of Chuangtzû*; and to Allen & Unwin and Dr Garma C. C. Chang for their kind permission to reproduce two extracts from Dr Chang's *The Buddhist Teaching of Totality: the Philosophy of Hwa Yen Buddhism*. I must also acknowledge my debt to Upasaka Lu K'uan Yü (Charles Luk), whose works, *Ch'an and Zen Buddhism* (three vols, Rider & Co.) and *Secrets of Chinese Meditation* (Rider & Co.) cover both Buddhist and Taoist meditation; and to Professor Chou Hsiang-kuang, whose *Dhyana Buddhism in China* (Indo-Chinese Literature Publications, Allahabad, India) contains valuable expositions of the meditation practices of several Chinese sects.

Note: My use of capitals or otherwise for certain words used sometimes in a mystical sense, such as 'Mind, mind; Wisdom, wisdom' may seem somewhat inconsistent, having been dictated by the requirements of the contexts in which they appear.

Only those foreign words which, unlike *Nirvana* and *karma*, as yet show little sign of being accepted into the English language are printed in italics.

Preface

The sacred practices of Chinese and Tibetan mystics constitute a fascinating subject at once too broad and deep to be covered in one book. Not daring to attempt a comprehensive, scholarly account, I have taken a very personal approach. As one who, moved by a lively interest in Eastern religions, has travelled extensively in China and on the fringes of Mongolia and Tibet, I have sought to describe something of what I found; for, amidst much that was merely colourful rather than spiritually inspiring, I came upon certain teachings and practices that bore witness to impressive soarings of the human spirit. As far as possible I have woven into my material stories heard and personal experiences so as to offer the reader a series of insights just as I acquired them by happening upon them here and there. Most of the book relates to what I learned during the two decades immediately preceding the 1949 communist revolution, which swept away the last fragments of many an ancient tradition. Though some of the stories recounted belong to a more distant past, that is because they were still current among my Taoist and Buddhist friends. My concern has been hardly at all with history, but with what I saw with my own eyes and heard with my own ears. Thus Confucianism, which by then had lost its unique position as the supreme guiding force to China's rulers, probably comes off less creditably than it deserves.

Almost a quarter of a century has passed since last I visited the mountain retreats described, so I cannot pretend to remember the details of my conversations with innumerable monks and hermits, some of whom became my teachers; but I do remember vividly their substance, so the words here put into their mouths more or less accurately reflect what they said. For the sake of brevity, I have sometimes attributed to one individual a sequence of remarks actually culled from several sources, in other words, I have exercised the writer's privilege of 'tightening up' his material – but not, I think, at the expense of essential truthfulness. Unfortunately, I have had to supplement traditional stories and accounts of personal experiences with a certain amount of exposition to give a more rounded picture of the various kinds of Chinese mystical endeavour; yet even the expository passages are based much more on what I heard and saw than upon my subsequent reading about the subject, so they are still largely first-hand.

The term 'mysticism' is frequently misunderstood and even confused with 'obscurantism'! I use it to mean all that pertains to the search for intuitive experiences inaccessible to ordinary understanding and to the merging of one's being into something so exalted, so vast as to be beyond all human conceptions of divinity. India, no less than China, has been a fount of Asian mysticism; my saying nothing of Indian mystics is due to my having travelled too little in India to be able to speak of them from direct observation. On the other hand, I have included some aspects of Tibetan mysticism in a book largely devoted to its Chinese forms for the very good reason that Tibetan and Mongol lamas were to be found in many parts of China and that many devout Chinese Buddhists looked to them as teachers.

Tense has presented a minor problem. So much of what I describe has vanished since the communist revolution and it is difficult to say to what extent certain Taoist and Buddhist practices have survived in Taiwan and among overseas Chinese communities. I hope my inconsistencies will be excused.

While writing all that follows, I kept in mind two kinds of reader: those whom I hope it will amuse rather in the manner of a travel book, on account of the exotic atmosphere it conjures up; and those who may find in it some inspiration to explore the marvellous realm of the spirit variously known as the One Mind, the Great Void, the Way. In the last chapter, I have ventured to suggest some ways of putting the teachings of

Chinese and Tibetan mystics to good account, although I recognise that they provide no remedy for ills afflicting people in the mass.

Autumn 1973   *John Blofeld*
                              '*The House of Wind and Cloud*'
                              Thailand

Contents

Chapter 1

The Wish-fulfilling Gem

In Buddhist circles in China and Tibet there are many stories current about a marvellous gem that, once located, fulfils its finder's every wish. This gem lies always close to hand; but all too many people resemble the prince who travelled across the world to find it, only to discover in the end that it was inset in the very pendant he had been wearing all the time upon his forehead!

To put it another way, the path that leads past heaven and far beyond the highest god-realms runs straight from the spot where we happen to be standing. It is mysterious and invisible to minds befogged by concepts such as good and evil, light and dark, going and arriving, self and other, is and is not. To perceive it requires the seeing beyond sight, the hearing beyond sound – a hard saying, yet in some circumstances simple.

There is a religion beyond religions which leads directly to the grasping of the wish-fulfilling gem. For want of a better term, it may be called the mystic's quest. He may believe in this god or that, in a multitude of gods or none at all and yet arrive at the truth that transcends all creeds. This truth is grasped when the mind in its stillness reaches the no-place beyond thought. Knowledge is discarded, wisdom remains. God and no-god are found to be identical. No mental concept is involved, only experience – a unique perception, joy-bestowing, that leads to imperturbable tranquillity, to recognition of the beauty inherent in every flower, in every grain of dust, cement or dung, and to unqualified liberation from the human state. Enlightenment, Attainment of the Tao, Union with the Godhead are but

B

high-sounding names – the experience is nameless, being luminously perceptible but utterly beyond description.

Mystics there have been in every continent throughout the ages, though seldom in great numbers. To discover the path that lies before one's nose, there should be no need to go to Asia. And yet? The grim technology now poisoning the world is surging there as elsewhere, but it is still rather easier to find accomplished guides in the East, even though it may soon be otherwise. For, whereas Christian and Moslem mystics have generally been looked upon askance by their co-religionists and not infrequently suppressed, Hindu, Buddhist and Taoist authorities openly proclaim the mystic's way to be the highest path of all. Not that most followers of those three faiths are practising mystics – finding the path and cleaving to it are much too difficult for that – but at least they are encouraged to recognise the mystical goal as the crown of man's endeavours. Those among them who extol the hidden way are not, as used to happen in Europe, hustled off to remote monasteries, there to be reverently regarded, but unobtrusively restrained from proclaiming a truth with awkward implications for established hierarchies. Buddhists, in particular, have been successful in evolving potent methods for hastening the mystical experience. (Nowadays even Catholic prelates occasionally seek their guidance with a view to reviving the languishing contemplative orders.)

Unfortunately, almost everything pertaining to mysticism lies beyond definition and description. Transcending logic, it deals with truth that is attainable only by direct intuition. Therefore did the Taoist sage, Laotzû, say of it: 'He who knows does not speak; he who speaks does not know.' Yet mystical experience is open to all who thirst for it. Whether as a result of teaching or of spontaneous intuition, it sometimes happens that a person tumbles into joyful awareness of the source of incomparable bliss that lies within himself. If a Christian, he may conceive of it in some such terms as sudden awareness of the immanence of God; others will interpret it in accordance with their varying traditions; but all who attain it are at a loss to communicate its nature in words. Perhaps I may be forgiven for paraphrasing a few paragraphs from a book I wrote on Tibetan mysticism, *The Way of Power*, as these, though still very far from expressing the mystery, come as near to it as I can get:

'*There are moments when a marvellous experience leaps into mind as though coming from another world. The magic that calls it forth is often so fleeting as to be forgotten in the joy of the experience itself – it may be a skylark bursting into song, the plash of a wave, a flute played by moonlight or the fateful shrieking and drumming of a mountain storm; a lovely smile, perhaps, or a single gesture, form or hue of compelling beauty; a familiar scene transformed by an unusual quality of light, or a cluster of rocks suggestive of beings imbued with life. Or the spell may be wrought by a sudden exaltation, a jerking of the mind into an unknown dimension. A curtain hitherto unnoticed is suddenly twitched aside and, for a timeless moment, there stands partially revealed – a mystery. This mystery has a hundred names, all of them inapt. It has been called the Good, the True, the Beautiful. Philosophers term it the Absolute; Christian mystics, the Godhead. It is the Beloved of the Sufi Moslems, the Tao of the Taoists and, to Buddhists, Nirvana, the Womb of Existence, Suchness, the Void, the Clear Light, the One Mind. Were it not that frequent and clear visions of it engender a compassionate urge to communicate its bliss, it would be best to use no name at all.*

Names set bounds. Unfathomable, the mystery can be intuited but never grasped, how then named? On mystics and poets, visions of it sometimes dawn unsought; hearty extroverts, if they glimpse it at all, are shocked into fears for their sanity and dismiss it as a mental aberration – or run for the doctor!

To say that it exists is to exclude from it the non-existent and limit it to what the speaker means by existence. To say that it does not exist involves the other side of the dilemma. Both concepts are too crude to describe its subtle nature. To say that it is pure mind is well enough in certain contexts, but it ought not to be set apart from matter with which it is inseparably united. However, man's consciousness cannot easily divest itself of symbols. Accomplished mystics therefore tend to describe it in terms of the qualities lent to it by the filter of their senses : Clear Radiance, Immaculate Void, Ecstatic Bliss, Infinite Love, All-Embracing Unity.'

Of one thing I am sure – a mystical experience, whether vague or intense, is nothing less than direct intuition of Ultimate Reality. Suddenly the universe is seen, as it were, in another focus; the myriad objects are recognised as being simultaneously many and One; all kinds of contradictions fall into place; tranquillity and joy supervene. All previous perceptions of oneself and one's surroundings are seen to have been blurred and distorted as if by a wrongly focused telescope; dimness having given place to blinding clarity, what once seemed commonplace presents a shattering loveliness. Even if the intuition is not intense, it will arouse a conviction that something mysteriously sublime lies beyond the scope of ordinary perception, something infinitely desirable which, if gazed upon for long, would miraculously reveal life's meaning!

The theistic term for it, 'union with the Godhead' strikes a nice balance between the Western conception of a supreme *being* and such Eastern expressions as the Tao, Nirvana, denoting not a being but a *state*. In any case, the affirmations of mystics of many faiths demonstrate quite clearly that the experience, except as regards its intensity, is the same, those who attain it being transported to a level at which distinctions such as 'being' and 'state', 'God' and 'no-God' are meaningless. Words, beliefs, conceptual thought are lost in the 'clear white light' of Truth. It follows that, between the theistic Western concept and the more impersonal Eastern concept, there need be no conflict, once it is accepted that direct experience is all that matters.

Interpretations of the experience vary not only between followers of the theistic and non-theistic traditions, but also among people belonging broadly speaking to the same tradition.

To most Taoists, for example, it is enough to experience direct communion with the Tao, without interpreting it at all; whereas Buddhists tend to relate the experience to their beliefs in reincarnation and in Mind as the only reality.

What is needed for entrance to the path is not a particular religion with this or that dogma, but simply a holy state of mind – a conviction that something illimitable and sublime lies beyond the realm of shifting thought and vision, something to be apprehended in the stillness of our innermost being. When a Taoist with his more impersonal conception affirms that 'all things come from the Tao, return to the Tao, *are* the Tao', and when a Christian declares that 'all things come from God Who, being omnipresent, permeates them all', both are pointing to the same inexpressible truth.

To pursue the path, what is chiefly required is a method whereby ego-consciousness and the coarse perceptions of the six senses (including mind) are progressively transcended. The initial aim must be profound inner stillness, for the chief barriers to attainment are the ceaseless waves of thought that distract the mind from its sacred quest. Hence Buddhists and Taoists have established techniques for controlling the mind's persistent wandering and for combating the restive assertiveness of the supposed 'ego'. In silence and stillness, perception is born.

Taoist mystical philosophy in the classical form first expressed in the works of Laotzû and Chuangtzû, pays little heed to the question of survival after death, being centred upon the attainment of profound tranquillity for its own sake. To the extent that those sages sought tranquillity without reference to a setting or ultimate goal, they may be described as quietists rather than fully fledged mystics, though their writings – especially Chuangtzû's – are too enigmatic to permit any certainty. However, whether or not as a result of Buddhist influence, there later developed in Taoist circles, side by side with the traditional quietism (and the popular search for a kind of physical immortality, which lies outside the scope of mysticism), thirst for a supremely transcendent goal – the achievement of perfect union with the Tao in which nothing remains of the individual seeker although, paradoxically, *nothing whatever is lost*! The one essential difference between this particular Taoist concept and that of Buddhism is that, whereas Buddhists, believing in rebirth, hold that failure to attain the goal must lead to further wandering through the realms of birth and death, the Taoist belief is that failure would entail a gradual disintegration of the spirit as final as that of the body.

Of the Taoists I met in the lovely hermitages scattered throughout the length and breadth of China and built in dream-like settings amidst bamboos and pines, rocks and peaks, streams and cascades, many were simple quietists. Individualists devoted to the doctrine 'let things and people be as they are', they seldom talked of aims. Given to an antique mode of dress and old-world courtesy, they were fond of smiles and laughter, gentle, full of humour and happy to beguile visitors with simple meals, mulled wine and as much good conversation, wry or serious, as one could wish for. I was repeatedly struck by their tolerance, their love of natural beauty and of simple, frugal things – above all, by their tranquil joyousness. How well they exemplified one of their favourite tenets, namely that true happiness has little to do with fame, prestige or riches. No wonder Confucians, republicans and communists in turn considered them dangerously subversive; for who, having tasted the joys of tranquil non-involvement, would willingly return to the onerous political, social and commercial responsibilities imposed by highly organised societies upon their members? Here, in summary, is a description of Taoist mystical belief: The Tao is infinite, eternal. It is not only the fount, but the container, the very being, the true non-substance of the universe. Putting aside all calculated action, all greed, ambition and similarly egotistic qualities, one should learn to intuit and live by nature's rhythms; to meet gain and loss, life and death with smiling acceptance; to cease interfering and let everything just be, welcoming all kinds of beings and circumstances as separate manifestations of the Tao, each with its own place and function; to enjoy the passing moment lightly for its own sake, savouring its special flavour with delight, but never forming attachments, much less giving way to passions. Living thus, attending to the inner silence, resting in objectless awareness, one gains imperturbable serenity. This in itself is enough.

Some Taoist mystics, going beyond this, would add: When serenity is won, one may gradually come so close to the mysterious Source that the blissful unity in the very heart of multiplicity is ever present to the inward eye. By submerging ever more completely in the light flowing from within and abandoning that wraith once mistaken for an 'I', one leaps beyond the world of form and, in this life or at death, enjoys such full communion with the Tao that the finite is lost in the infinite where, far from being diminished, the small becomes co-extensive with the vast, and thus the great transmutation is achieved.

Yet, despite the captivating qualities of Taoism, it is mysticism in its Buddhist form that has always appealed to me most and, as I am writing largely from first-hand experience, it will have a larger place than Taoism in all that follows. In China up to the middle of this century, there were thousands of Buddhist temples and, especially in the lush central provinces, not a few large monasteries. Their lovely curling roofs rose amidst the suburbs of ancient grey-walled cities, peeped from groves clinging to mountain slopes, or were mirrored in the waters of willow-fringed lakes, for Chinese Buddhists shared with Taoists a love of natural beauty. In the border regions, where the temples were often built in Tibetan style, the people – whether Mongol or Tibetan – were Buddhist almost to a man, unlike in China proper where people with Confucian leanings and adherents of the folk religion greatly outnumbered Buddhists.

In essence, though not necessarily in practice, Buddhism is a wholly mystical religion. To understand Chinese and Tibetan meditational and other yogic practices, it is necessary to have some knowledge of Mahayana principles. From my first teachers I learnt to distinguish between two levels of truth, two levels of experience – relative and absolute. At the former, such pairs of opposites as 'self' and 'other' are indubitably real; at the absolute level no such dualism obtains and nothing separates 'self' from 'other', since no entities are possessed of anything in the nature of 'own being'; all forms, being transient as dreams and unable to exist independently of one another, are ultimately void. Experience of this higher level, I was told, is attended by great bliss; beholding the Great Void confers no vista of dreary emptiness, but a glimpse of the unutterable perfection that lies beyond all colour, shape and other marks of being. Yet neither aspect can be divorced from the other, both being true embodiments of reality. To remain at the level of relative truth is to be sunk in unending delusion; to exist wholly at the level of ultimate truth is to be lost in bliss at the selfish cost of renouncing kinship with the myriads of beings still tossed upon the ocean of alternating life and death, and blind to an equally valid aspect of reality. For, when the limitations of logic and conceptual thought are transcended, reality is discovered to be *simultaneously* One and many! Enlightenment consists not in passing from here into Nirvana, but in recognising that this every-day world is simultaneously Nirvana, thus no passing is involved, but a new mode of perception, a seeing with new eyes.

My Buddhist teachers used many synonyms for the Tao to suit different contexts – the Womb of Dharmas (entities), to signify the one container of the many; the Great Void, to indicate the essential voidness of the myriad entities, not one of them possessed of 'own-being'; the One Mind, to bring home that the world of form consists of dream-like phantasms brought into being by undifferentiated Mind's creative play; or the Buddha-Nature, meaning that state of perfection inherent in all beings that is experienced upon Enlightenment. The term One Mind was frequently used in connection with meditation, the aim of which is to become liberated from the delusion of there being 'self' and 'other' through direct intuitive experience mentally attained. By mind is delusion created; by mind, overcome. By mind is man bound; by mind, set free.

In speaking thus, my teachers emphasised that all such terms and explanations inevitably do violence to the beauty and perfection of what Is, dragging the Nameless down to the level of philosophy and metaphysics. 'There are times', they would say, 'when the sight of a flower or the sound of a raindrop plopping into a pool tells you more of reality than all the words in the gigantic K'ang Hsi Encyclopedia; but, until intuition arises in your mind, words will have to do.'

Every step along the path brings an increase in wisdom – which has nothing whatever to do with knowledge. To hasten its coming, one must close the doors of the six senses and cultivate the objectless awareness that arises when thought is stilled. Side by side with wisdom must compassion be aroused, this being the remedy for wisdom's chief opponent – the concept of 'I' and 'other'. Methods of stilling the mind form the principle support of the Wayfarer. Some of these may at first sight seem bizarre – childish, even. Broadly they can be divided into 'self-power' and 'other-power', though meditation teachers smilingly explain that these two are the same. Since the effort to acquire wisdom must be made by the seeker himself, help from outside – whether human or divine – is of no avail; hence the term 'self-power'. Nevertheless, since the seeker is not really separate from the Source, the wisdom that wells up in the stillness is also 'other-power', an inflow from what, at the plane of relative truth, is termed 'without'.

Since what is to be cultivated is not knowledge but a state of mind, very varied means can be used. To some of these, a scholar with no mystical leanings – say, a biochemist – might perhaps accord a certain grudging respect as 'psychological techniques'; others would be bound to excite his derision and yet be none the less effective. People with a pietist turn of mind and those whose strength of 'feeling' exceeds their aptitude for 'thought' are taught to conceive of the One Mind much as though it were a celestial being – a transcendental Buddha – and of the streams of power which radiate from it (dividing, sub-dividing and becoming increasingly individualised the more the level of relativity is neared), as Buddha and Bodhisattva figures. The subtle aspects of Ultimate Reality, being beyond the range of conceptual thought, can be apprehended at the earlier stages only through symbols of one sort or another. What struck me as strange at first, though I find no strangeness in it now, is that even one who *knows* that the Bodhisattva figures personifying wisdom, compassion, skilful action and so forth are but symbols for the realities they represent, benefits, nevertheless, from meditating on them *as if* they were in truth the beings depicted. This being so, it ceases to be surprising that people who do in fact believe in them as celestial beings tend to be just as successful in reaching the goal as those who utterly discard anthropomorphic symbols.

As one of my teachers put it: 'Just as the city of Peking can be reached by those who take the right road to it, whether they call it Peking, Peiping or Yenching, so can realisation be attained by directing the mind to it unerringly, whether the seeker conceives of it as I Hsin (the One Mind) or Amitabha Buddha (the celestial Buddha of the Pure Land).'

As to the apparent plurality of the celestial Buddhas and Bodhisattvas, I remember a revealing little Tibetan story. Once a simple-minded devotee of Avalokitesvara (personification of Compassion), cast down by failure to attain realisation despite years of meditating on that Bodhisattva's form, ran to his lama and exclaimed: 'If in spite of my devotion, this book I am holding drops to the ground when I let it go, I shall turn from one who has filled my mind for years and cleave to Manjusri (personification of Wisdom) instead.' The book did not fall, being caught up by a sudden manifestation of Avalokitesvara; but, even as they watched, that exalted being's garb and features underwent a change and he now became Manjusri! 'Well', remarked the lama, laughing, 'what are you gawking at? You surely did not suppose that Avalokitesvara and Manjusri are different beings?'

An important Buddhist tenet is the doctrine of rebirth. It is held that unskilful (i.e. wrong, deluded) actions, words and thoughts forge chains of karma (inexorable consequences) which lead to aeon upon aeon of wandering in the realm of birth and death. Since life here is inseparable from pain, frustration and general unsatisfactoriness and since many life-courses must be run before an opportunity of attaining liberation comes again, there is a sense of urgency about making good use of the present life. However, this urgency apart, doctrines concerning the nature of life after death have little to do with the quest for mystical realisation – a state which naturally transcends all doctrines. Whereas the reality of the goal is beyond doubt, the way in which it is fitted into the adept's own creed and the manner of interpreting it are matters of belief that vary from one individual or community to another.

Thirst for realisation may be aroused by direct intuitive experience or by confidence in the wisdom of those who affirm its reality. Also, one may judge the tree by its fruits. Besides reading some impressive accounts of European mystics, I have been privileged occasionally to meet Chinese and Tibetans far advanced along the way. Always they struck me as lovable people whose very presence was a source of happiness. Spontaneous, merry, tranquil, kind, these accomplished adepts may be taken for simpletons by one unfamiliar with the signs of attainment; their wisdom is not worldly wisdom and they behave in ways startlingly different from conventional notions of sanctity. Incapable of being perturbed by anything thought to happen on earth, in heaven or hell, they are at once too light-hearted to appeal to solemn churchmen and too indifferent to life's ordinary concerns to impress the worldly. But for their poignant sympathy for less fortunate beings, nothing would have power to mar their inner joy. I cannot be sure that I have ever stood in the presence of a fully Enlightened being, since those who have attained that state are the last to proclaim it; but, during my wanderings in China and the Tibetan border regions, I met several people who possessed in varying degrees the qualities I have described. So moving were such encounters that, even had I known nothing of the path those sages trod, I should have reflected that whatever it was that had made them the men they were must surely be more precious than anything else in the world! Alas, such sages have always been rare. That I had the good fortune to encounter several was due to my spending a lot of time seeking out contemplatives, often in remote and solitary places. Naturally they were greatly outnumbered by co-religionists more concerned with pietism or propitiating gods and demons than with pursuing the arduous path to mystical attainment.

Buddhists and Taoists, though they do not hold the universe to be the creation of a supreme deity, have a lively sense of the existence of hierarchies of supernatural beings. Whereas it is rare to find a Westerner who, having repudiated the notion of a creator God, yet clings to the biblical belief in the hosts of heaven and hell, in East Asia just the contrary holds true. The Confucians, while generally conceiving of Heaven (T'ien), the king-pin of natural moral order, as impersonal, had no doubt as to the existence of invisible hierarchies, though they heeded the advice of Confucius to leave such beings respectfully alone. Similarly, Taoists held the Tao to be impersonal; even the Jade Emperor, a deity believed to preside over an infinite number of gods, spirits and demons, was thought to be created by and subordinate to this impersonal principle. According to the Mahayana Buddhist doctrine, there is no God and the universe, being the creative play of Mind very imperfectly apprehended by the senses, comes close to being illusory; yet, insofar as humans can be said to exist, so, too, can gods and demons; but they, like men and animals, are subject to decay, death, rebirth.

If the notion of 'no God but many gods' seems odd, the oddity lies largely in the English language which, except for the use or omission of a capital G, makes no distinction between two entirely different concepts. Whether or not the universe is the creation of a supreme deity is one question; whether it contains mysterious orders of finite beings normally imperceptible to man is quite another. Fortunately I need not undertake to substantiate the reality of gods and demons, as they have never been of much concern to true Wayfarers since they can neither help nor hinder the quest for mystical attainment; from that standpoint, their existence or non-existence is as irrelevant as that of fish or insects!

In a quite different category from either God or gods are what are known as the *celestial* or *meditation* Buddhas and Bodhisattvas, such as Amitabha Buddha or Kuanyin. Among Chinese Buddhists there are two (sometimes overlapping) explanations of these beings. According to one school of thought, they are not really beings at all, but personifications of phenomena too mysterious and abstract to be conceived of except by means of symbols; personification of the wisdom-energies flowing from the One Mind is held to be one of the *skilful means* for leading people towards Enlightenment. By meditating on such embodiments, one is led to acquire the quality of wisdom, compassion or skilful action as the case may be, thus hastening progress towards realisation. Among Tibetan Buddhists, the use, as aids to meditation, of anthropomorphic symbols representing all the energies both 'good' and 'bad' within the adept's personality has been very highly developed. According to the other school of thought, the meditation Buddhas and Bodhisattvas are real beings who, born into this or some previous aeon, have attained liberation but compassionately renounced Nirvana's bliss so as to remain within the universe for the purpose of ferrying other beings across the bitter ocean of delusion. In practice, such distinctions do not matter. Meditation on Amitabha or repetition of his name accompanied by one-pointed concentration produces the same result regardless of the adept's concept of his nature. The quest for intuitive wisdom requires not *knowledge* but a *method*. A drowning man does not need to know how air originated or its chemical composition, but an effective method of getting it into his lungs! Were his conception of air's nature completely wrong, he would benefit from breathing it no less than a physicist or chemist caught in a similar predicament. With the revealed religions it is vitally important to believe that Jesus or Mohammed actually existed and taught eternal verities; were it possible to prove that the founder's existence was a myth or that his doctrine had no divine basis, such religions would break down or have to be utterly transformed; though, to the Christian or Moslem *mystic*, a discovery of that kind would make no essential difference.

Naturally I did not stumble upon advanced mystics as soon as I arrived in China; nor, had I done so, should I have known what to make of them. The next chapter describes the everyday religious scene as I found it. It forms the background wherefrom the shoots of mystical endeavour rose like occasional fine trees amidst an ordinary rain-forest.

Chapter 2

Remnants of the Three Teachings

In 1933 I arrived in China as a very young man all agog to
experience wonders and delights. Happily I found them in
plenty, though in forms that were seldom close to my imagin-
ings. In particular, the religious scene was as colourful as could
be wished, but it took time to discover the remnants of beauty
and wisdom that lay behind a façade of all-too-human gods and
laughably ugly demons. There was not much to suggest their
presence; the Chinese I met were, with a few notable exceptions,
either heirs of the old Confucian agnosticism or holders of a
hotchpotch of beliefs that struck me at first as being more
picturesque than uplifting. However, I soon came upon one
endearing trait, a genius for harmonising any number of conflicting doctrines. Of intolerance there was none. Confucian-
agnostic husbands lived happily with vaguely Buddhist or
Taoist wives and thought nothing of it if some of their children
contracted Christianity at school. Nor were those same
agnostics averse to buttering up gods or placating demons now
and then, for all that they spoke of such beings as the product
of peasant superstition. It was bewildering.

'Mr Chang, are you a Confucian?'

'Naturally. The sage Confucius shaped our government,
education and way of living for around two thousand years. All
of us are Confucians at heart.'

'Buddhism does not appeal to you, then?'

'Indeed it does. Shakyamuni Buddha taught how to escape
from aeons of wandering in the world of dust. I am devoted to
his teaching.'

'At all events, you are not a Taoist?'

'Why not? The Taoist sages were adept at living in accord with nature, indifferent to loss and gain. And some Taoists are wonderfully skilful in teaching how to achieve a joyous and vigorous old age. Look at our poetry and painting and you will see we are all of us Taoist in spirit.'

'Ah yes; but, philosophy apart, doesn't offering incense and petitions to the gods of mountains and of rivers, to deified generals, imps, sprites, demons and the rest, make you smile?'

'One may smile, but it is just as well to be on good terms with all sorts of beings. A good many of them enjoy roast chicken and a few cupfuls of wine more than the fragrance of incense – those things have more body to them.'

'And what of ancestral spirits?'

'Naturally one sweeps their tombs at the Pure Bright Festival and makes offerings before their spirit tablets at the proper times. Otherwise they would feel neglected.'

'So, in fact, you subscribe to four or five religions?'

'What a strange way to put it! Why reject anything that cannot be known for certain? Each of the Three Teachings – Confucianism, Taoism and Buddhism – is admirable in its way. As for making offerings to spirits and ancestors, who knows whether they are there or not? If they are, they must find the offerings pleasing. If not, at least the living are edified by such rites, do you not think?'

Such tolerance made a refreshing change from the sectarianism at home in England which had so often been the cause of malice, slander, pain and bloodshed. All the same, with my Western background, I boggled at some of the contradictions involved. For example, a Buddhist friend, just back from paying respects to the spirit tablets of several generations of his ancestors, readily affirmed that the departed usually reincarnate within forty-nine days of dying.

'But how, then, can those who died decades ago be present to receive your offerings?'

'Who can be sure that they are not? Perhaps a man has

several souls. One might linger near his tablet to enjoy our filial piety, surely?'

This open-mindedness was reflected in the obsequies accorded to the dead, especially during the seven times seven days succeeding their demise. Before the spirit tablet would be set offerings of food and wine in the Confucian tradition; Taoist and Buddhist monks would be invited in to perform rites turn by turn; and, very occasionally, a Christian pastor would be asked to pray for the dead man's soul – just in case! This last, however, involved deception as even a Chinese pastor could not be depended upon to do his part if he knew his 'rivals' had had a hand in the care lavished on the departed. Chinese Moslems and Christians were alone in not sharing the tolerant attitude that was otherwise universal among their countrymen.

The people I have called agnostics were largely to be found in government offices and schools. Their modern education had made them too wary of 'retrograde superstition' to care for any religious label, but they generally retained the Confucian notion of a heaven-directed moral order. Whether Heaven (*T'ien*) was a being, a state or just an abstract principle had always remained vague and the failure to distinguish between 'spiritual' and 'material' had been castigated by Christian missionaries as evidence that the Chinese are incorrigible materialists; but it is more likely that the Confucians resembled Taoists in holding that everything in the universe is compounded of spirit. I believe that was the general Chinese view, in which case the worldly appearance of the deities of the folk religion, who were depicted as being close celestial counterparts of Chinese officialdom, had nothing to do with materialism. The proposition that heaven and earth must be much the same since 'matter is essentially spirit' is very different from its Marxian opposite, namely that mind or spirit is a product of matter.

On the whole, I was not greatly impressed by what I saw or heard of Confucianism. Theoretically it sounded admirable, especially the doctrine that man's first duty is to rectify himself and persuade others to do the same, so that families become rectified and, in turn, the state. Nor, on the face of it, can any fault be found with the teaching that the five great virtues are benevolence, rectitude, propriety, wisdom and good faith; and that five relationships should be observed with loving concern on the one side and loyal obedience on the other – those between father and son, ruler and minister, husband and wife, elder and younger brother, friend and friend. It was also taught that ancestors should be honoured and other spirits left respectfully at a distance. Thanks to Confucianism, from 106 A.D. to 1905, all but the lowest ranks of officials were selected by public examination, thus making status dependent on learning and ability and allowing individuals from the humblest classes to rise to lofty heights. Well and good, but the power of rulers, fathers, husbands became virtually absolute as a result of rigid observance of the five relationships; women's status was not enviable; and the emphasis on propriety led to extreme conservatism and to disproportionate importance being accorded to intricate ceremonial.

The better side of Confucianism is illustrated by the story of the philosopher Mencius's mother, a poor widow who thrice moved her dwelling so the boy would be near school and subsequently admonished him for truancy by tearing the cloth she was weaving so as to make him realise that neglecting his studies was tantamount to destroying the fabric on which their very existence depended. There is also the story of the filial son who lay each evening upon his parents' bed so the mosquitoes, surfeited with his blood, would leave the old couple to sleep peacefully. But emphasis on filial duty could also have ugly results. When China was still governed as an empire (up to 1911), there were many cases of cruel severity such as that of a young man who, shocked by his younger brother's refusal to lend money to their father, threatened the boy with a knife and earned such a scolding from the parent he had been trying to help that he actually dared shout back. For this offence against the Confucian code, his father buried him alive and was later acquitted on the ground that a parent reviled by his son was entitled to slay the offender!

That this appalling aspect of Confucianism in practice lived on well into this century was brought home to me when I was living in a rented apartment in Kunming. Not long before, my landlord's daughter, on failing an examination, had poisoned herself, leaving behind a letter in which, after tenderly expressing gratitude for her parents' care, she asserted that, by making such poor use of the money spent on her education, she had forfeited the right to live. My landlord, I am sure, sincerely mourned her, but so great was his pride in her filial devotion that he had had the letter framed and hung for his visitors to see! No wonder the Taoist sages spoke chidingly of Confucian harping on the virtues of loyalty and filial piety.

The quotation from the Confucian Analects which runs, 'If his mat was not straight the Master would not sit,' gives only some idea of the lengths to which the Confucians carried their notions of propriety. A young friend of mine, brought up in the aristocratic quarter of Canton, told me that, in the late 1920s while accompanying his father on visits to former imperial officials, had he failed to remember such details as which foot to raise first in crossing a door-sill, the family would have been covered in shame. Every step, every gesture was rigidly governed by antique protocol; if invited to sit, he had to perch bolt upright on the edge of the chair, ready to spring gracefully to his feet whenever someone deigned to address him. Doubtless such formality had elegance and even beauty. Even so! As for women, one lady told me that, in her family, it would have been unthinkable for the womenfolk to go to bed before her grandparents had retired; worse still, they had to pass the evening *standing* in the old people's presence!

The Taoist tradition was very different. The communities of hermits I visited, though ceremonious in their conduct towards strangers, by no means held that strict observance of decorum is essential to the regulation of society. On the contrary, they chiefly valued spontaneity; it was their aim to let everyone be exactly as he is, to allow beings to take care of themselves as effortlessly as forest trees. As for obedience to authority, loyalty, filial piety and the rest, they felt there would be no need for them among men living in intimate accord with nature. Animals looked tenderly after their young without giving a thought to benevolence. Enacting laws was a sure way of creating criminals, whereas if people were persuaded of the folly of accumulating property, coveting useless luxuries and craving for rank and status, crime would vanish and judges and policemen be able to stay happily at home 'nourishing their vitality'. In a joyfully ordered society where greed and ambition were unknown, who would wish to rob, deceive, make war?

Much as I loved my Taoist friends, I did find their philosophy somewhat impracticable. Well suited to poets, philosophers and mystics, it seemed unlikely to succeed with ordinary people of our day and age, unless they were taught it as children and lived out their lives in small, self-sufficient communities. A good many Taoist hermits were engaged in fulfilling the religious needs of the peasants who supported them. To the pantheon of gods and spirits inherited from the ancient folk religion had been added a curious assortment of deified mortals. At the apex of the whole were such beings as the Jade Emperor, the Royal Mother of the Western Regions and Laotzû himself in deified form. These illustrious dignitaries presided over a hierarchy governed by the divine rulers of various celestial and terrestial regions; it included star-gods, deities belonging to each small locality, nature deities and many, many more. I came to understand that, to those who set store by divinities, these beings mattered greatly; whereas, by those with deeper understanding, they were not disbelieved in but respectfully ignored.

In Taoist hermitages could still be found recluses who cultivated the Tao by seeking, through a process known as the 'internal alchemy', to create within themselves the embryo of a spirit body into which they could pass at death. This, as I afterwards learnt, involved a yogic process that included

contemplation, breath control, muscular movements, visualisation and – in some cases, already very rare – sexual intercourse,
all aimed at manipulation of three energies, spirit, generative
force and breath-cum-cosmic-force. But there were others who
held that the 'internal alchemy' really pertained to an esoteric
means of obtaining communion with the Tao. Also, there were a
few Taoists who employed the 'alchemy' with the intention of
becoming so immersed in the Tao that the last remnants of
duality between the transient individual and the Ultimate
Source would vanish. These were the true Taoist mystics.

Of considerable interest were the magical aspects of Taoism
comprising relatively mundane matters such as divination,
evocation of spirits, exorcism and the miraculous cure of
diseases. Not all of this was mumbo-jumbo; I was able to
observe Taoist recluses functioning both as physicians and
'psychiatrists' with considerable success, besides some more or
less convincing evidence of supernatural beings. That there are
demons I no longer doubt, though I cannot be sure whether
they are of a different order from phenomena widely known also
in the modern West, such as the 'mental factors' which cause
people to behave in ways quite out of keeping with their characters, as when a crowd of normally well-meaning individuals is
swayed to commit horrifying brutalities, or when someone is
afflicted with what (without really knowing much about it) we
term psychosis or schizophrenia. Other examples include those
beings who appear in visions and startlingly vivid dreams and
those who plant in our minds the sudden intuitions often
attributed to 'second sight', 'the voice of conscience', 'guardian
angels', 'God'.

The flavour of popular (as opposed to quietist or philosophic)
Taoism can best be conveyed by a few stories of a kind in which
notions derived from the ancient folk religion predominate.
They are on a completely different level from the higher flights
of Chinese religious thought, but picturesque enough to have a
certain charm.

A silk merchant surnamed Tsêng who dwelt near Chiuchiang

brought seeming misfortune on himself by being in a hurry. While sailing up river past Dragon Pool Uncle's gorge, he forbade his boatmen to halt and pay their customary respects to that deity. At night a storm arose, flooding the hold to the ruin of his bolts of silk and satin. What is more, Dragon Pool Uncle was heard to say in a voice of wind and thunder: 'To old Tsêng, a ten-year sentence for discourtesy!' Thenceforth the merchant's business fell away; unused to poverty, his principal wife soon went to the Yellow Springs (died); his favourite concubine took to peddling her charms on a flower-boat where those with a grudge against Tsêng laughingly sought her favours; and his children left for the city where they were glad to take what menial tasks they could find. As to Tsêng himself, he became a wandering beggar and endured hardships for many years. One showery day, happening upon a shrine dedicated to Dragon Pool Uncle, he sought to pass the time by repairing its leaky roof. While gathering flat stones for this purpose, he came upon a jar protruding from the mud which proved to be full of silver taels. Using this treasure to advantage, he gradually re-established his fortunes and was able to reassemble the remnants of his family and even to replace his two lost wives by taking to himself two young orphans who were sisters. Yet, as his wealth increased, his contentment waned and he grew nostalgic for the days when his worldly goods had been no more than a set of ragged garments, a bamboo pillow and a dilapidated paper umbrella. Deafened by the wrangling that went on among his wives and children, he put on his oldest clothes, slipped out into the night and walked all the way to Mount Hêng, where he settled as a Taoist hermit. Now he began enjoying wealth of another kind, the song of the wind in the pines, the silvery gleam of a waterfall, the pearl and coral of sunset clouds, none of which occasioned him a moment's anxiety. Living to a ripe old age, he would reply to those who asked his name: 'I am Dragon Pool Uncle's debtor.'

Another story concerns the Viceroy of Liangkuang from whom a pair of palace eunuchs had extorted huge sums as the price of not whispering certain matters into the ear of their Imperial Master. At his wits' end as to how to recoup these sums, the Viceroy had a certain Taoist brought down from his mountain retreat to whom he gave orders to set about transmuting base metals into gold. 'Do as I require', he said softly, 'lest it come to my mind that a hundred strokes of the heavy bamboo is the one ingredient lacking!' To put off the evil day, the unhappy sage presently offered the Viceroy two ingots of gold that he had secured in his sleeve before setting out with his guards for the viceregal palace in the City of Rams. Concealing his excitement, the Viceroy observed gently: 'Very good, but you must speedily transmute a hundred times that quantity or who knows to what measures I might reluctantly be forced?' To their next meeting the Taoist perforce came empty-handed and, to put himself once and for all beyond the Viceroy's power, cried out some treasonable slogans invented by the T'aip'ing rebels, thus incurring the penalty of death. When confirmation of his sentence arrived from the capital, he was publicly beheaded; whereupon, to the onlookers' amazement, from the blood spurting from his torso rose a cloud white as a lustrous pearl, in the heart of which was seen the spirit-body of the Taoist dressed in resplendent robes and reclining nonchalantly upon a couch. The Viceroy, repenting of having caused the death of a man so manifestly holy, erected a handsome shrine to which he daily repaired to offer the illustrious spirit prayers couched in elegant poetic diction which, inscribed by his own hand in scholarly caligraphy, were wafted heavenwards in the sacred fire. It is recorded that the late Taoist, being amply content with his immortal state, disdained to punish his former persecutor; indeed, the spirit and the living man became fast friends and collaborated in the composition of many a charming poem.

A third story concerns an occurrence in the reign of the Tao Kuang Emperor. Some local gentry of Tsohsien in the province of Shantung, happening to have a grudge against a jolly peasant familiarly known as Bully Tu, bribed the magistrate to condemn him to death for a murder they themselves had instigated. While the Emperor's confirmation of the sentence was being awaited, the prison cells resounded with the unfortunate man's protestations until, one night, he managed to attach his girdle to a beam and hang himself. On his body was found a paper inscribed in his own blood accusing the magistrate and five of the neighbouring gentry of having conspired to cause the death of an innocent man; and it was said that some of his fellow-prisoners had heard him vow to be reborn as a demon lusting to avenge the crime. A year later the magistrate, on learning that his old father had passed away, requested the customary leave of absence in order to observe full mourning. Riding towards his native district in the company of two mounted lictors, he presently rode into a thick mist, whereat the lictors by some mischance lost sight of him. Not knowing what else to do, one galloped forward and the other turned back. This second man was destined for a shock. Coming upon a patch of watery sunshine, he was just in time to see his master lifted from his horse by a gigantic figure whose lineaments, except for their huge size, resembled those of Bully Tu! Before he could either intervene or flee, the magistrate was swung into the air and dashed down with such ferocity that his skull cracked like an egg against the granite paving stones! Thereafter, two of the local gentry named in Bully Tu's indictment met with a rather similar fate and the three survivors, locking themselves in their homes, sent an urgent petition to a hermit on Mount T'ai who enjoyed wide renown as a vanquisher of demons. The next time Bully Tu's shadowy bulk reared up before an intended victim, the hermit, miraculously perceiving the scene from his mountain abode, uttered a magic formula which instantly transported the demon into his presence. 'Well, Bully Tu', he exclaimed, 'you really ought not to be so vengeful. Though innocent of the crime those people put upon you, you must surely have committed other bad deeds or fate would have treated you more kindly. You had best stay with me for a while and receive instruction concerning the Sublime Tao. Your being disembodied will prove no inconvenience and, if you are diligent, who knows? Ten years from now you may have become a cloud-riding immortal able to exist on dew and moonbeams and free to fly at will among the stars.' Full of eagerness, the demon contracted its wraith-like form and entered a gourd attached to its new teacher's belt, wherein it dwelt happily during the period of instruction.

Such stories, for all that they throw no light upon the beauty and sublimity of Taoism in its higher forms, do give an idea of the colourful background against which Taoist mystics pursued their exalted quest. It was the popular aspect that one met on every hand; the other being more rare and, to some extent, hidden. It is the nature of true mystics not to proclaim their talents or in any way draw attention to themselves; for, with spiritual progress, the desire for fame fades. Who, on discovering the truth of 'not-I', would so nullify that attainment as to say '*I* have attained it'? In the realm of mysticism, self-proclaimed attainment is a sure indication of fraud or self-delusion!

Like Taoism, Buddhism, which was introduced into China some two thousand years ago, offered a vista of all kinds of practices and beliefs ranging from the realm of folklore to the highest spiritual level. A characteristically 'Chinese Buddhism' had gradually evolved, its form much influenced by Taoism, its content remaining faithful to the Mahayana Canon which, over the centuries, had been translated from Sanskrit into Chinese (and also into Tibetan). The many sects into which Buddhism had been divided in earlier times had largely merged. Both in China and Tibet, 'belonging to such-and-such a sect' had come largely to mean receiving teaching transmitted down a certain line of teachers, rather than that one upheld or emphasised a particular set of doctrines or methods to the exclusion of others. In practice one made use of whatever method seemed best suited to one's temperament and abilities. However, in the sense of there being six different sets of methods based to some extent on different sections of the doctrine, it could be said that, during the years I spent in China, some six sects were in existence. As they still continue in Hong Kong, Taiwan and among overseas Chinese communities, one may speak of them in the present tense.

The Pure Land Sect (Ching T'u Tsung) stresses faith and compassion and presents a special yogic method of reciting, with deep concentration, a single sacred formula.

The Ch'an Sect (more widely known outside China by its Japanese name, Zen) sets little store by painstaking study of doctrines, preferring the method of direct experience achieved through meditation based on what may be only a limited knowledge of doctrine. (Logically it is at variance with the Pure Land Sect in that it stresses 'self-power' as opposed to 'other-power' attainment; but, among Chinese, these have generally been recognized as two aspects of a single 'power'.)

The Hua Yen Sect stresses the interpenetration of all entities and the ultimate unity of fact and principle; its practice combines intellectual understanding with meditation.

The T'ien T'ai Sect is syncretic and seeks to embrace seemingly conflicting schools of thought (including Confucianism). Stressing that entities are simultaneously possessed of form and void, it has developed a very important meditation system of its own.

The Esoteric Sect (Mi Tsung) attaches equal importance to doctrine and yogic meditation. In some respects, it is more Indian than Chinese in form, having been re-introduced into China from Tibet after the demise of the more characteristically Chinese sect of that name.

The Pure Consciousness Sect (Wei Shih Tsung) is intellectual rather than devotional or experiential in its approach. Though emphasising that the only reality is consciousness, it nevertheless treats of consciousness as being composed of 'seeds' or monads.

The supreme aim of the exponents of all these practices and doctrines, with the possible exception of those who advocate the Pure Consciousness philosophy, is the same – attainment of the mystic's goal. Institutionally, the sects were long ago combined

in a uniquely Chinese way, with most monasteries engaging in
Pure Land devotional rites, Ch'an (Zen) style meditation, and
studies (sometimes meditations, too) pertaining to the doctrines
of all the sects. Only the Esoteric Sect tended to keep apart;
mainly because, in the form in which it had survived, it
depended for instruction upon Mongol or Tibetan lamas more
often than upon Chinese monks.

Most of what I have to say about the practices of the various
Chinese sects will be found in the appropriate chapters. Alas,
it is impossible to do justice to the tremendous richness of
Chinese Buddhism, whose splendour is reflected not only in its
exalted mysticalpractice and profound philosophy, but also in a
wealth of art treasures, especially poems, paintings and sculpture.
Like Taoism it flourished most widely, however, at the popular
level and was similarly, though to a slightly smaller degree,
influenced by the folk religion. The following is fairly typical
of the stories told by those pious Buddhist laymen who were
more at home with miracles than with the difficult task of
spiritual cultivation.

The sacred mountain Wu T'ai is believed to be under the
patronage of Wênshu (Manjusri Bodhisattva), personification
of the Buddha-Compassion. Among the many tales of miraculous occurrences there is one about a small girl who came with
her parents on a pilgrimage. Piously they climbed each of the
five sacred peaks on foot instead of riding comfortably on their
mules. On approaching the south peak by a narrow precipitous
footpath, they came upon a beggar standing at a point where it
was difficult to ignore his importunity. Whereas the parents
brushed past him quickly with averted eyes, the little girl
stopped to speak kindly. 'You', said the beggar, 'will enjoy a
fine spread when you reach the monastery up there. I hope you
will spare a thought then for one who has not the price of a
maize-cake or bowl of thin soup.' Knowing her sleeve-purse
was empty, the child impulsively handed the poor old man her
only ornament, a thin silver ring, saying: 'Don't worry, Uncle.
This should buy you a good dinner.' In a flash the decrepit

figure was transformed into a radiant being who, returning the ring with a smile, prophesied that this generous child would enjoy great good fortune in the years to come. The 'beggar', being none other than Wênshu in disguise, this promise was most amply fulfilled; besides marrying well, the girl became a poetess of some renown, being favoured alike by gods and men.

At a different level is an anecdote in the Ch'an (Zen) style relating to my stay in a hillside monastery near Kunming's lovely Êrh-hu lake. One evening while chatting with a young monk who often visited my cell, I heard a tapping on the door. Calling out 'Who is it?', I walked into the corridor outside, only to find it deserted. Naturally I was puzzled, until my young companion said: 'Your question must have driven him away.' Then I understood. During meditation periods in that monastery, we used to work upon the conundrum 'Who am I?', systematically stripping away each layer of the ego in the hope of achieving direct perception of our true nature, wherein there is nothing that can rightly be called 'I'. My caller had demonstrated that the only possible Ch'an answer to 'Who is it?' is 'No one'! Incidentally, the Abbot of that monastery had taught me the same lesson on the day of my arrival. Having asked my name and been told it, he had rather brusquely remarked: 'While you are here, please look hard for the *owner* of that name!'

By Buddhists at all levels, the fact of rebirth was taken for granted. Testimony to that phenomenon is provided by many striking stories, of which the following is characteristic: In the Meihsien region of Kwangtung province lived a couple surnamed Ch'ên who lost their son at the age of seven during a smallpox epidemic. Overwhelmed by the tragedy and recalling several warnings that their dwelling stood upon a site that was geomantically ill-omened, they moved away to another part of the village, blaming themselves for not having done so in time to avert the child's untimely death. Nine years later, they received a visit from a stranger whose speech proclaimed him to be a native of Ch'aochou, a district lying at some distance from their own. Without as yet explaining the purpose of his visit, this stranger rather pointedly observed: 'I fear there has been some mistake. I made sure I should find you living in a house overlooking the village well through windows glazed with mother-of-pearl.' Casting an uneasy glance at his wife, Mr Ch'en replied that they had indeed lived in such a place but had moved away following upon a family tragedy. At these words the stranger's face lit up and he continued: 'And was there not a pumpkin patch in your garden, with a pig-sty just beyond it? There was? Excellent. Permit me, then to tell you my purpose in coming here to pay my respects.'

He had come to that part of Meihsien and sought out the Ch'ên family as a result of the strange behaviour of his nephew, a nine-year-old child nick-named Little Three. For several years now, the boy had frequently upset his elders by talking about a couple he insisted were his 'other parents'! Also he claimed that his surname was not really Yuan, but Ch'ên. No punishment had been found to cure him of his obstinacy and at last his father, noting the consistency of his seemingly fantastic assertions, had begun to take the matter seriously. Thus encouraged, the child had described in great detail the house and village where he claimed to have 'lived in a previous life', mentioning particularly the mother-of-pearl windows overlooking the village well, the pumpkin patch and the lean-to where pigs were kept. After many enquiries, the uncle had been directed to this village and, from what he had seen of it, it corresponded closely to the one described – which was strange indeed, for the little boy had never in his short life been in this part of the country, nor even met anyone from Meihsien who might have told him about it!

Eagerly Mr Ch'ên supplied the exact date and hour of his son's death, which proved to have taken place some nine months before the birth of the other little boy! Full of wonder, the visitor promptly invited the Ch'êns to accompany him back to the Ch'aochou district and see the child for themselves. This they gladly agreed to do and, although no advance notice was sent of their coming and no mention made of their identity, no sooner did the child see them walking towards his house than he ran out excitedly to greet them, crying 'Mama! Papa!' which, strangest of all, he pronounced in their own Meihsien dialect! As a result of all this, the two families became great friends and neither couple resented the child's affection for the other.

During my years in China, I heard many such stories, some of them no less circumstantial; I even met two or three people who claimed that, as children, they had remembered many details of their former life. Most of these stories had had one notable feature in common, namely that these people, in their previous existence, had died in childhood. I cannot recall even one satisfactorily circumstantial account in which this feature was lacking. This suggests that such memories are carried over only by those whose former lives were cut short at a tender age.

Having taken these rather inadequate glimpses at the popular religious scene in pre-communist China, we may now return to the subject of mysticism so as to review the methods used for cultivating intuitive insight into the true nature of being. If some of the methods to be described seem not far removed from the realm of folklore and superstition, it should be recalled that sophistication and learning generally have nothing to do with mystical experience; and that the yogic techniques employed were intended to suit people at every level from wholly illiterate to highly intellectual.

Chapter 3

The Path of Observation and Acceptance
Taoist Quietism

Even in the old days before the revolution, the Moon Terrace Hermitage had few visitors. The steepness of the rugged ascent and the distance from the nearest township were not in themselves enough to discourage pilgrims; for many pious people thought a pilgrimage hardly worth making unless it involved hardships. Under different circumstances, old ladies with the tiny bound feet once known as golden lilies would have been eager to make the journey, even though it would have taken them days to hobble and, if need be, crawl from the nearest spot that could be reached in a wheeled conveyance. Besides, it was always possible to hire light contraptions of bamboo resembling primitive sedan chairs and be carried up into the mountains on the shoulders of two or three bearers only too glad to strain heart and lungs for the sake of a few coins. No, the reason was that the hermits, though never failing in courtesy to those who came, disappointed many visitors by offering nothing at all in the way of spectacular religious rites; even on great feast days such as the Summer and Winter Solstices, no more than two candles flickered upon the altar and pilgrims who wished to burn incense were left to do so by themselves – with no music, no special rites – much as if they were at home kneeling before their household shrines. Word had spread that the hermits, albeit simple, blameless men, were lacking in piety to the gods and more likely to be found basking lazily in the sun than on their knees before the altar.

Much that I had heard made me determined to see the place. I found that its isolation and the difficulty of the ascent had not been exaggerated. From Kanhsien I went by river-boat for the best part of two days' journey, walked for two days through rice-fields set among gently rolling hills and came at last to a range of low mountains where the soil was so poor that the terraced fields upon their slopes had long since been abandoned. Following a rocky watercourse the rough path began to rise abruptly and, thereafter, there was hardly a level stretch. Panting and sweating profusely, I pressed upwards among those jagged rocks regretting the curiosity that had driven me to seek out a hermitage built among hills that were harsh and arid by the lush standards of that province, where copious sunshine, warm gentle rain and mists like soft white silk bring all things to fruition.

Presently I changed my mind. On the middle slopes, tall feathery clumps of grass grew amidst the lifeless rocks and wastes of pebbles. Higher still, there were groves of pine-trees and the rocks, whether less sheltered from the prevailing rain-bearing winds or better shaded than those lower down, were green with moss. The further I climbed, the more my surroundings came to resemble a lovely Chinese landscape painting. For once the path rose gently until, turning a bend, I came upon a rampart of tall, dark rocks rising from the gently sloping ground and mounted by a steep flight of irregularly spaced steps. These rocks, besides being almost black, were pleasingly grotesque in shape and honeycombed with holes and crevices to which clung all manner of mosses and small alpine plants, startlingly green against the sombre rock-face. The steps were massive; I had to place both feet on each before attempting the next. They led to an undulating spur admirably suited to a fortress, being hemmed in on two sides by perpendicular slopes, on the third by a deep gorge where thundered a mountain torrent, and on the fourth by a steep drop, so there was no possible access other than by the great steps I had just climbed.

With its back to the upper slope of the mountain stood the hermitage, a cluster of low grey-tiled roofs interspersed with pines and cedars and surrounded by an irregularly shaped wall of brick that rose and fell in curves like a dragon's back. The buildings looked immeasurably old and sombre, but not forbidding; there was charm about the contours of those heavy, slightly upturned eaves; and a harmony, though no obvious symmetry, about the way the buildings were spaced. No windows broke the surface of the outer wall, just a gateway like an elongated lychgate closed by two solid wooden panels covered with smooth black lacquer. The only spots of bright colour were a green and white *yinyang* symbol some two feet in diameter that split in half when the gates were opened and a horizontal board bearing the legend YÜEH T'AI TAO YUAN (Moon Terrace Hermitage) inscribed in green caligraphy.

After knocking for some time, I was admitted by a short, bright-eyed old man, bearded and clad in rustic Taoist garb – a sort of cap of sky-blue linen with a hole at the crown to make room for his top-knot, which was secured by a thick wooden peg; a loose gown of the same material and cloth sandals with thick straw soles. I judged that these garments were home-made and that even the material had probably been woven from local flax by the recluses or their attendants. As was the custom, we exchanged many low bows, each clasping his own hands and ceremoniously pumping them up and down with arms extended. Amidst an unhurried exchange of compliments, we enquired each other's name and I learnt to address him as Hsüan-ku Tao-jên (Recluse of the Dark Valley). The buildings were grouped about small courtyards. Leading the way to one that was entered through a vase-shaped opening in a dividing wall, he ushered me into the first of several small cells, each dimly lighted by a papered lattice window flush with its doorway. There was just enough space for the narrow curtained bed, a chest for belongings, a very small table and a single chair. On the bed were clean, gaily coloured quilts and a pillow stuffed with some sort of grain or seed that emitted a sweet fragrance. The old man murmured something and vanished, but soon returned with a tea-pot in a quilted basket, a handleless cup,

D

lidded and resting in a boat-shaped saucer, and a plate of sweet rice-flour wafers. He was presently followed by a lad dressed in a bronze-coloured costume similar to his own, who brought in a copper handbasin of warm water, a face-towel and – to my great surprise – an unused cake of expensive English soap which, judging from its tattered wrapper, had been hoarded through the years for some special occasion. If so, how kind of them to bring it out for me – a barbarian and one too insignificant to merit such attention! Unwrapping the soap, I sniffed its pleasant odour and lathered my face with it liberally, my appreciation winning pleased smiles from them both.

Having pressed upon me two cups of tea and several rice-flour wafers of a kind impossible to crunch unless first dipped in the hot tea, the Dark Valley Recluse took me on a tour of the precincts. No one else was about, the other hermits being variously occupied with meditation, gardening, gathering herbs higher up the mountain or just strolling about its slopes enjoying the evening sunshine. The courtyards were rather similar to one another, but each contained one or two fine trees and a different arrangement of flowering shrubs in pots, a miniature rock landscape or an ornamental pool with water-lilies. There were only two spacious chambers – a low-ceilinged hall used as a refectory and for such rare assemblies as a community consisting of only seven recluses and three young boys found necessary, and a chapel or small temple over which Tsang Ô, Goddess of the Moon, presided. She was depicted by a rather shabby but delicately carved and painted wooden image as a lovely maiden sitting indolently upon a couch. From her languorous pose, one might have supposed her a voluptuary, sister to Venus, but her cool and rather haughty virginal expression was that of a being remote from human passions. Closer to the back wall and to either side, were smaller images depicting Laotzû, a slight bearded figure grasping a horsehair whisk of faded scarlet, and the Immortal of the Crooked Pine, founder of the hermitage, who seemed to have succeeded in distilling the elixir of eternal youth, for he was represented as a handsome, slim young man with a pink and white complexion and eyes that glowed with mystic ardour. Struck by the air of neglect hanging over this small temple, I recalled having heard that these recluses were little given to ritualistic practices; and I was to learn that such rites as they did perform on appropriate occasions were motivated more by a desire to maintain tradition than by a pious attachment to any of the three divinities. 'We celebrate the birthday of the Moon Goddess with a certain pomp', one of the hermits was to say to me, 'but then, you see, our retreat was built in her honour and it would not be fitting to ignore the wishes of our founder.'

Soon after sundown the recluses gathered in the refectory where the three young boys – half pupil, half servant – were waiting to serve evening rice. Dark Valley now introduced me to his colleagues. They received me with a flurry of bows and smiles, each paying me some graceful compliment. One praised my fluency in Chinese, another my courtesy in condescending to visit a remote community of 'woefully undistinguished persons', and so forth. Though intended to make me happy, their exquisite politeness proved embarrassing as I was hard put to it to think of suitably elaborate replies. But I need not have been anxious, for the Abbot, smiling broadly at my halting attempts at elegant Chinese diction, gestured that we should take our places at table and, as though by magic, formality was banished. Right up to the time of bidding me farewell several days later, they treated me with the simple courtesy that springs from true concern for the comfort and convenience of a guest.

The food, though frugal, was tasty and we each drank a few tiny cupfuls of mild wine before rice was served about half way through the meal. My bearded companions (almost all Taoist recluses, old and young, wore beards and high-piled hair) seemed delighted to have a foreign guest and made no difficulty about answering any of my questions. Concerning the origin of the community, one said:

'In the old days our retreat belonged to some adherents of Heavenly Master Chang's sect who successfully practised all

kinds of magic healing and yogic exercises. Then, towards the
end of the late Manchu dynasty, the authorities disbanded
them claiming that they were shamefully licentious. It was the
usual kind of misunderstanding that arises whenever the green
dragon white tiger yoga is cultivated simply because female
partners are required. Officials are so ignorant about these
things. Happily, two very elderly recluses were allowed to
remain on undertaking not to transmit the secrets of that yoga.
Now, these two old men were not especially interested in yogas
of any kind, so the undertaking was readily given and presently
they attracted, by ones and twos, a small band of scholarly
disciples more concerned with harmonious living than with
fashioning spirit bodies for use after death. Ever since then, our
hermitage has been the resort of people like that. Most of us at
this table have been officials or merchants in our time; dis-
gusted with a world of cruelty and greed, we came here to live
in a manner hardly possible to city dwellers or people bound by
family responsibilities. All we desire is to cultivate joyful
tranquillity and thus live to a ripe old age, hale and vigorous
to the last.'

'And have you found tranquillity?' I asked wistfully. For
answer came a smile that illumined the faces of the listeners.
There was no need for words.

After evening rice, tired out by the strenuous climb, I went
straight to my cell and scarcely had time to sniff the pleasant
fragrance of my pillow before falling fast asleep. The next
morning, after breakfasting off millet gruel mixed with savoury
titbits, I set off with the Dark Valley Recluse to explore the
neighbourhood. The hermitage, as I have explained, was
situated on a spur of gently undulating ground close to the
mountain-face. In front of it lay what might be called a natural
garden, that is to say, no attempt had been made to convert
the spur into a garden proper and yet the features of this
seeming wilderness had beauties too refined to be wholly the
work of nature. The rocks protruding from the ground were of
such pleasing shapes and so richly garbed in moss and trailing

lichens that I soon began to suspect nature had artfully been helped to give of its best. The gorge where flowed a swift and thunderous torrent was certainly nature's handiwork and so perfect in itself as to require no improvement, but elsewhere things had an air of having received delicately concealed attention. The trees – mostly pines and cedars – disposed their limbs in ways either charming or amusingly grotesque; and there were dells containing just such a wealth of harmoniously contrasting shapes and colours as one would expect to find in an old and well-kept rockery. Yet one had to look carefully to become aware of a subtle human artistry cunningly disguised.

'It seems that yesterday I climbed further than I knew, for this is surely heaven,' I remarked, bringing a gleam of pleasure to the old man's eyes.

'Ah, you have noticed our hidden garden,' he replied. 'People coming from the cities generally have eyes for the torrent and for that vista of hills stretching beyond – you will agree they are lovely and you should come here in the evening light when the sun drops behind that blue range – but they seldom notice what lies close at hand, never guessing that centuries of loving care have gone into the making of this hidden garden. Nature, so harmonious in the large, is often careless and untidy in the small. Rocks may occur too near together or too far apart. Trees in their eagerness for what sun and shade they need may overreach themselves, causing a certain lack of harmony and balance. These little oversights can be redressed, but it would not do, I think, to create a palace-style garden on a remote mountainside such as ours. All that is needed is a lightly guiding hand. When contemplating a little change, it is fitting first to observe what you wish to alter at different times of day throughout the four seasons of the year, lest by hasty action something precious be lost. Also you need to become a rock or a tree yourself before you can judge how to make a change that will accord with its nature.'

'*Become* a tree?'

'Do you find that astonishing? If you had much time, I

would show you. You just sit before it in sunshine and in cloud, in rain or snow if necessary, and project your mind into it. Slowly you learn how to be at one with it, to sense its rhythm, to know how its branches would dispose themselves under just slightly altered circumstances. Only then can you make a change without doing violence to its treeness. All good gardeners get to know their plants as intimately as their own children; otherwise how could they be *good* gardeners?'

'I see. But what about rocks, mountains, streams? How can one know them like children? They have no life.'

'Do they not?' exclaimed the old man in real surprise. 'How strange you should think that! Everything is formed by the sublime Tao. Everything *is* the Tao. How then can some things have life and others not? To an insect that lives a single day, a human may seem an object immemorial; yet you and I know that human life is short; to us it is rocks and mountains that seem eternally unchanging. But are they so? Are not their comings and goings as dreams in comparison with the innumerable aeons between the birth of a universe and its ending? And if by life you mean consciousness, how can you tell that rocks are not conscious? Those who know them intimately recognize that they have not only consciousness but moods – gloomy and menacing one day, relaxed and smiling another.'

I did not gainsay this. After all, how *do* I know that rocks lack consciousness? I have read of English people who believe that flowers are happy and bloom more charmingly when they know they are loved. Why then not rocks? Who has the knowledge to draw such distinctions with authority?

The following days passed enchantingly. The recluses, besides meditation, had no set practices and, living in so remote a place, they had plenty of opportunity for that, so they were by no means averse to my spending as much time with one or another of them as I wished. One old gentleman, the Cloud Ocean Recluse, confided that he had formerly been a banker. 'All that plotting and scheming to pile silver upon silver, just think of it!' he exclaimed. Weary of a life so niggardly in terms of leisure and peace of mind, he had left his sons in charge of the family fortunes and, 'wandering across mountains and rivers' for a year or so, had come upon the Moon Terrace Hermitage where he had settled happily among kindred spirits.

'People are blind to their own good,' he told me, glancing smilingly around the modest cell which contained all that remained of his once considerable possessions – books, two or three wall-scrolls, some good vases and a set of unusual caligraphic implements that included a brush-rest of translucent jade carved to resemble a three-peaked mountain. 'From childhood one is led to believe that wealth is what matters most, so we slave long hours each day to accumulate more of it, forgoing all sorts of pleasures in pursuit of what is wrongly assumed to be pleasure's source. How topsy-turvy that is! As Laotzû says, those who fill their houses with gold and jade have to stay in all day to look after them. We bankers certainly know all about that! Assets need more attention than an old man's teenage concubines to prevent them from flying away. Nor is that all. Because I was wealthy, merchants and officials used to invite me to feasts that followed in such quick succession that my stomach rebelled at the very sight of rich food. My wives, my children and nephews were at loggerheads with one another, each trying to win my favour at the expense of the others. The women especially were insatiable for more silks, more jewels and novelties with which to dazzle people as stupid as themselves. Leisure, tranquillity, simple affection – everything worth having was sacrificed on the altar of Ts'ai Shên (the God of Wealth). When I spoke to my sons of the wisdom of frugality, pointing out how much richer they would feel if they learnt to have few wants, they surely thought I had gone mad.'

'Well, having never been wealthy, I shall take your word for it that wealth is a curse, but I doubt if the sufferings of the rich are harder to bear than the miseries of the needy.'

'Poverty! No one who has seen the faces of poor farmers when they are compelled to sell their children or watch them starve can think lightly of poverty. We Taoists see no virtue in

that, but we do believe the secret of happiness lies in learning to
have few wants. A simple dwelling, a few sets of garments to
suit the changing seasons, plain food tasty enough to tempt the
appetite – these are all that is needed for tranquil living. If
people were content to have no more, there would be so much
to share with others that stark poverty would become rare. A
hideous evil of modern life is the war waged on simplicity by
investment agents, promoters, advertisers and their kind who
deliberately arouse a never-ending succession of new wants so
that people will forever be dissatisfied with what they have and
strive all their lives to acquire new possessions at no matter
what cost in health, energy and leisure. No wonder Laotzû
sternly enjoined rulers to discourage the production of geegaws,
teaching that "loss brings gain; too much of anything,
confusion".'

At the word geegaws, my eyes strayed involuntarily to the
luxurious array of writing implements so much at variance with
the simplicity of his cell – the jade brush-rest, the exquisite
porcelain water-jar, the delicately scented ink-slab embossed
with gold characters, the engraved flat stone for grinding the
ink and the cylinder of ruby-red porcelain from which rose a
forest of fine writing brushes of many shapes and sizes. Guessing
my thoughts, he burst out laughing.

'No need to be extreme, dear friend. These things, though
workmanlike in being admirably suited to their purpose, are
luxurious and expensive. But then, we Taoists dislike imposing
strict rules – even on ourselves. Such rules as we choose to live
by are never strict and a rare indulgence here or there does no
harm to those with wisdom enough to keep things within
bounds. Even our Abbot, a truly abstemious man and lover of
simplicity, prizes the set of jade wine-cups given him by a
grateful pupil – not for their costliness, I assure you, but for the
beauty of their texture and lovely sheen. If a few costly trifles
come our way – I brought these writing implements from my
old home where I left almost everything else I owned – there is
no harm in treasuring them, provided there is no attachment.

I mean, suppose the Abbot's cups were stolen, one cannot even imagine him sadly repining their loss or taking pains to acquire another treasure in their place. Life brings what it brings and one learns to accept its gifts and withdrawals – including death itself – with equanimity. When the peonies or chrysanthemums bloom, I enjoy having a vaseful on my table here, but I certainly do not hanker after them when they are gone. So it should be with all precious things.'

His speaking of rules had introduced a new train of thought and I enquired: 'You said just now Taoists are not fond of rules, but does this community live without them?'

'Not altogether. Since we eat together, we observe fixed times for taking rice. And, though we weave our own cloth from flax obtained together with most of our food from the tenants in the valley where we have land endowments, we are not altogether self-sufficient, so there are regular duties connected with provisioning, gardening and so on. None of them are onerous, nor is there the least compulsion. Systems of rewards and penalties create more trouble than they dispel. Even to cherish notions of duty and virtue is harmful, since, by defining "right", you set up the category "wrong". Where there is wisdom and tranquillity, people do what is needed spontaneously, not wasting a moment on such thoughts as "I shall be praised or get into trouble if I do this or that" or "I *must* do this and must *not* do that because the one is right and the other wrong". Groves of trees and flocks of animals, having no rules, are not burdened by police, armies, magistrates and tax-collectors, yet they fulfill their needs as well as circumstances allow. So it is with us. We live by the principle of *wu-wei* (non-action), that is to say by avoiding action that does not arise spontaneously from present circumstances. So though rules govern our eating times and the days for heating water in the hermitage bath-house, we have not a single rule to govern the all-important matter of the manner in which we cultivate the Tao. Performing whatever studies and meditations we wish, we are guided by whatever teachings and teachers we choose. As it happens, I like to spend most of the night in meditation contemplating the Tao which shines forth in the secret chamber within, but were I to sleep all night and all day, no one would chide me.

'The younger recluses here and the three young boys receive teaching from us elders. Good, but we do not set about it by laying down what they, as Taoists, must study. Instead, we start by observing our pupils, leading them on to reveal what is in their minds and to display what talents and bents belong to them naturally. Then, by whatever means come to hand, we guide each along the lines he is best fitted to follow, often learning more than we impart. What wonders would be wrought and what tragic failures avoided if schoolmasters did the same! Sooner or later, our pupils come to study the works of such sages as Laotzû, Chuangtzû and Liehtzû – not because they must, but because they grow curious about the sources of our ideas. If they had no tendency that way, the young recluses would not have come here in the first place. Even so, just *how* we teach them depends not on our own preferences but on the pupils' natural aptitudes and inclinations. With the three boys who serve us, it is different. Such boys come here because their fathers, poor farmers, vie to send their sons to a place where they will receive an education as well as wages. All three of those we have at present are bright boys and, when they know enough to be able to read ancient works fluently, they may be eager to study our Taoist classics. If not, no one will mind and we shall gladly help them to find different kinds of opportunities elsewhere.'

'I wish I could stay here long enough to learn even one part in eight of what they will learn', I observed sadly. 'Could you not somehow summarise your teaching? It would be a precious gift to take away from here.'

He gave me a warm smile, but answered modestly: 'An ignorant old fellow who has spent half his life as a banker is not the best person to instruct you in the mysteries of the sublime Tao. You had best ask His Reverence the Bamboo Pin Recluse. A homeless one since childhood, he is a veritable cloud-riding immortal, one who "lives on a diet of moonbeams and dew", as the saying goes.'

The recluse he spoke of was a middle-aged man with a strikingly bushy beard, whom I had found smilingly taciturn during the conversations that took place at mealtimes.

That evening, wanting to think over all the things of which Dark Valley had spoken, I strolled out to a rocky perch overlooking the noisy, foaming torrent to watch the sunset. A shower of rain had deepened the colour of the rocks and scattered jewels upon the foliage. A sharp breeze blew from the west. The setting sun cast its light upon massed banks of cloud, dyeing them with glorious tints – coral, crimson and gold. The rushing water, blue mountains and majestic clouds and the beauties of the 'hidden garden' combined to stimulate awareness of the workings of the mysterious Tao, mother of everlasting change. The rapid transformations of the clouds were a reminder that the seemingly eternal mountains were, however slowly, undergoing transformations no less stupendous. Clearly the founders of the hermitage had not erred in choosing to contemplate the Tao in this magic spot where nature's unending dance was presented in such dramatic form. Here the world of corrupt officials, money-grubbing merchants and gun-toting policemen seemed as far off as another planet. Living a few years in this place and using one's eyes, one might stumble upon the innermost secrets of those bearded sages without so much as leafing through their ancient books.

Driven back to the hermitage by darkness and a sudden freshening of the breeze, I heard from somewhere the music of an evening rite. To the accompaniment of gong and cymbals, two voices were uplifted in a strangely haunting air, melancholy and yet evocative of sweetness and tranquillity. Chilled by my vigil on the rocky perch, at evening rice I drank gratefully of the mulled, herb-scented wine which was the nearest thing to a luxury in the daily lives of those abstemious men. Presently I caught the eye of the Bamboo Pin Recluse and, addressing him as Your Immortality, a Taoist term indicative of great respect, and asked if I might visit him after the meal. Hitherto, not a little intimidated by his air of remoteness from human concerns, I had scarcely exchanged words with him, so his eyes betrayed a flicker of surprise as he answered courteously: 'By all means. We shall drink tea from the plants that now grow wild on the southern slope of this mountain. One of the pleasures of visiting out-of-the-way places in this part of the country is tasting the local teas, infused, of course, with local water. Taken away and brewed elsewhere, they never taste as good.'

His cell was much like the others. At first sight, the tea-things he brought out looked coarse and rustic, but the loving way he handled them suggested they were old and in some sense precious. The rough glaze ended in an irregular line far from the base, as though thick honey had been poured onto unglazed earthenware from above. The tea itself was honey-coloured, slightly bitter but with a strange and attractive fragrance. Since it would have been discourteous to come straight to the subject of my visit, I found the tea-things a pleasant subject for con-versation. The tea-pot, I learnt, though generally similar in appearance to the cups, was unworthy of notice, whereas the cups were a family heirloom, not only very old but replicas of a form so ancient that the world's first tea-drinkers might be presumed to have used cups much like them.

'I am fond of them', remarked my host, 'because they symbolise what Laotzû calls the uncarved block – a man or object in its natural state, moulded by the Tao, unsophisticated, holy. They are, as you see, close to being "uncouth", a word sometimes used of our great sages. We modern Taoists – I mean those during the last thousand years or so – are, to my mind, over-ceremonious and too fond of tradition for its own sake, whereas the sages of old were, to quote from the Tao Tê Ching, "as simple as babes", their manners "as artless as the uncarved block". It also says: "Ceremonious behaviour betokens lack of oyalty and good faith".'

Presently an opportunity arose to beg him to expound some-thing within my comprehension of the mysteries of the Tao.

'Mysteries?' he answered, laughing. 'Viewed properly, every detail of life, of nature, is a mystery as profound as any you can name, so how should our doctrine be especially mysterious? Let me tell you what we do here in our community – *not do* might be a better term for it, since a distinguishing characteristic of Taoists is refraining from all calculated action, responding only to the needs of the moment. The essence of our belief is summed up in a few sentences from the Tao Tê Ching: "The universe had its beginning in what is called the mother of the universe. Know the mother, that you may know the child. Know the child, that you may return to and hold fast to the mother; then, as long as life lasts, nothing can harm you." The mother is the formless Tao; the child is the Tao of a myriad transformations. Or, as Laotzû puts it: "Voidness is the name for that in which the universe had its origin; actuality is the name for the mother of the myriad objects. Therefore, empty your minds to view the secret source; and observe actuality in order to view its manifestations. These two arise together, though separate in name. Both are mysterious – mystery upon mystery! Such is the gateway of all secrets!"

'I shall explain. Voidness and the actuality one sees all around are simultaneously one and the same. Therefore, to know the undifferentiated source of the myriad objects comprising actuality, one must sometimes empty the mind of thought and sometimes contemplate the world of form. Neither has meaning apart from the other. To fix the mind always upon emptiness would be to become like wood or stone. To keep it always upon the form realm would be to behave like a simpleton who mistakes dreams for reality. We are not philosophers lost in speculation. Bandying metaphysical arguments is not our way. Direct perception takes the place of concepts. Now we rest in the mother, the pure undifferentiated Tao; now, in the child, observing the rhythms of the seasons, the objects of nature, the flux of change in which our lives are passed. Learning to dwell above duality, we perceive no contradiction between the void which is also form and the form which is also void. Thus we come to know things as they really are – void, yet capable of taking countless forms; possessing form, yet intrinsically void. Secure in this knowledge, we view gain and loss, meetings and partings, the rise and fall of circumstance, life and death with cheerful equanimity. What then can harm us? If the omens point to one's living another twenty or thirty years, well and good; if death must be faced tomorrow or today, well and good. But it is useless to know this from hearsay or from a book as one knows that in Kiangsi province there are twenty-seven different species of dragonfly. You must open the inner chamber of your mind and experience it there as you experience the sun's heat or water's wetness *by direct perception*!

'How then to set about this? First, by paring away wants and superficialities of every kind as so much useless baggage; and also by following a simple régime free from poisons to mind and body, that you may enjoy unending health, energy and mental clarity. Anxiety, covetousness, irritation recede as wants grow fewer and energy increases; thus the first taste of tranquillity is won. In tranquillity, the mind perceives its inner stillness; contemplate that stillness that you may attain perception of the all-pervading void. Yet, since voidness is not truth if the non-void is excluded, alternate the hours you spend in inward contemplation with hours spent in observation of the myriad processes and forms, noting how each comes into being, waxes, wanes, decays and passes on. Neither withdrawing the mind from things, nor content to accept them as they appear to eye, ear and touch, come to know them as they are. Alternating periods of meditation with gardening or with culling herbs and studying their healing properties is a way we favour. Landscape painting is another, since it involves a union of without and within. The painter observes mountains, oceans, trees, rocks until he has gained such an all-embracing knowledge of their nature that, unless his hand wants skill, he can scarcely err in portraying them; yet he does not seek to reproduce what he sees, but conjures other formations forth from the voidness of the mind, while taking care that they are true to nature. Those unskilled in painting often contemplate rocks or trees with another purpose, that of causing the mind to enter its object and intuitively sense its thusness. Once intuition dawns, the sight of bees at work among the flowers will produce the taste of honey as surely as if it lay upon the tongue.'

The Bamboo Pin Recluse gazed at me thoughtfully as if to gauge how much I had understood.

'How I envy you!' I said. 'It is lovely to live in this place, free from all desire for fame and power and wealth and happily content with simple things. And what a boon to be so imperturbable that the imminence of death and the prospect of continuing this idyllic life for many years to come are equally welcome! But what comes after death? The body, I know, decays; its juices nourish the grass on which other creatures feed and so on in a perpetual cycle. Is there also spirit? Do you aim, like certain other Taoists, at achieving immortality?'

'Why aim?' he laughed. 'What would be the use of that? If there is a spirit apart from the body, it will undergo cycles of change just like flesh and blood and everything else, whether one *aims* at that or not. If there is no spirit, what good would aiming do? Faced by this unresolved enigma, as in all other circumstances, it is best to reflect that things always take their natural course whether one likes it or not. Having aims does not affect them one way or the other. Besides, since nothing within the realm of form remains without change even for a moment, what is the difference between mortality and immortality? The juices rising from your grave to feed the grasses will no longer be *yours*; why should any spiritual residue you may have be otherwise? Suppose you have a spirit destined to exist for aeons, since it can never cease changing, for how long will it be *your* spirit? Believe me, dear guest from the Western Ocean region, nothing is gained by speculation. Things are always as they are. Learning to accept whatever comes is the only gateway to tranquillity.'

So saying, he fell silent and, after a little while, I rose to take my leave.

'I am grateful, Immortality, for your patience. Two days from now I must leave you to resume my life in the city. I had been dreading that, but now you have shown me the folly of regret. Since all things are as they are and will be as they will be, regretting some and welcoming others is but to hurt oneself without making any difference to what happens.'

'Just so,' he replied. 'May your journey prosper.'

Two mornings later, almost the entire community came to the gateway to see me off, bowing and pumping their clasped hands in amiable farewell.

In describing this particular Taoist community rather than another, I have sought to depict Taoism in its quietist form. Taoist magical practices do not concern us here; and, as for fully fledged Taoist mysticism, which is concerned not just with tranquil living of this life but total immersion of the immortal spirit in the Tao, it is so close to the mysticism of Ch'an (Zen) that what is said in a later chapter of the mystical practice of that sect applies to both. Indeed, many scholars hold the view that Taoist mysticism in its most developed form is a direct (if unconscious) borrowing from Buddhism. In any case, it is certain that Ch'an (Zen) Buddhism, for all its doctrinal fidelity to the Mahayana canon, is in many ways the child of a marriage between Buddhist and Taoist thought; for much more than a thousand years, the two faiths have interacted to such an extent that, at least where mysticism is concerned, there is no essential difference of approach. On the other hand, the kind of quietism illustrated in this chapter is uniquely Taoist.

To provide a historical perspective for what has been said about Taoist quietism, I shall quote three short passages from Burton Watson's lively translation of the Book of Chuangtzû and relate a charming anecdote told me long ago by a Taoist friend.

The first of these passages from Chuangtzû contains a paradox that is typical of the kind found in the writings of many a quietist and mystic. Though there is a precious goal to be attained, the approach to it must be effortless. Striving is not the way. Such a paradox cannot be solved at the level of logical thought since, logically speaking, any attempt to get somewhere involves an element of striving.

'The formless moves to the realm of form; the formed moves back to the realm of formlessness. This all men alike understand. But it is not something to be reached by striving. The common run of men all alike debate how to reach it. But those who have reached it do not debate, and those who debate have not reached it. Those who peer with bright eyes will never catch sight of it. Eloquence is not as good as silence. The Way cannot be heard; to listen for it is not as good as plugging up your ears. This is called the Great Acquisition.'

Now follow two exhortations to inward-turned contemplation which Chuangtzû put into the mouths of certain mythical characters:

'The essence of the Perfect Way is deep and darkly shrouded; the extreme of the Perfect Way is mysterious and hushed in silence. Let there be no seeing, no hearing; enfold the spirit in quietitude and the body will right itself. Be still, be pure, do not labour your body, do not churn up your essence, and then you can live a long life. When the eye does not see, the ear does not hear and the mind does not know, then your spirit will protect the body, and the body will enjoy long life. Be cautious of what is within you; block off what is outside you, for much knowledge will do you harm. Then I will lead you up above the Great Brilliance, to the source of the Perfect Yang; I will guide you through the Dark and Mysterious Gate to the source of the Perfect Yin.'

'. . . You have only to rest in inaction and things will transform themselves. Smash your form and body, spit out hearing and eyesight, forget you are a thing among other things, and you may join in great unity with the deep and boundless. Undo the mind, slough off the spirit, be blank and soulless, and the ten thousand things, one by one, will return to the root – return to the root and not know why. Dark and undifferentiated chaos – to the end of life none will

E

depart from it. But if you try to know it, you have already departed from it. Do not ask what its name is, do not try to observe its form. Things will live naturally and of themselves.'

The anecdote once told me by an old Taoist runs thus: The Ch'ien Lung Emperor was fond of travelling about the empire, sometimes in disguise. Once, dressed as a scholar of moderate means, he put up at an inn in a lakeside village not far from Hangchow. Here he chanced to meet a Taoist recluse who had called in for tea and a bowl of noodles on his way back to the monastery where he dwelt. This recluse, taking the Emperor for one of those Confucian scholars who used to set up schools to prepare candidates for the civil service examinations, engaged him in conversation. The Emperor, entering into the part expected of him, brought forth a number of Confucian adages on the subject of loyalty, filial love and the rest with all the bombast of a self-esteeming pedagogue, until the Taoist interrupted him by exclaiming: 'Really you Confucians make too much of those trifles. You chatter of virtue as if you knew all about it, but how can there be virtue unless one keeps silent and contemplates the sacred Source of Being lying within the secret chamber of the mind? "Talking is easy; doing, hard," as the saying goes.'

Taking this as a slight on the great Confucius, the disguised Emperor bridled and said tartly: 'What has silent contemplation got to do with it? That is an old excuse for sitting down and doing nothing, leaving others to toil for the welfare of family, community and State. You would be just as well occupied lying on your back and snoring.'

'Aha!' cried the Taoist, 'here we have a pretty fellow who talks of toiling when it is quite clear he has never had a speck of good brown earth beneath his inch-long finger-nails! As for me, I tend the gardens of our monastery for hours each day. Look, my hands are cracked and my fingers gnarled with toil.'

'Then I am glad to have met you,' replied the Emperor, recovering his good humour. 'Your garden does you credit.

Yesterday I saw for myself how handsome the peonies look in the great courtyard of the monastery. Still, good gardener though you be, you ought not to pretend that sitting and contemplating your inner being has anything to do with it. You will not persuade me the flowers are the more beautiful and luxuriant for that!'

'Indeed they are!' exclaimed the Taoist indignantly. 'Flowers respond to those who tend them with a proper knowledge of nature's ways and that comes from contemplation of the Tao. If you do not believe me, try growing some yourself. Talking to them of loyalty and filial piety will not help matters. You will soon see the difference.'

At this the Emperor, recalling the glory of the palace gardens in Peking, smiled and said: 'Well, as it happens, I do have peonies at home and I would say their splendour has no equals in the world!'

'What boastfulness! You will have to let me see them, unless you choose to be taken for a liar.'

'Insolent Taoist!' roared the Emperor, shouting for his attendants and no longer caring to conceal his identity, 'you have called the Son of Heaven a liar before the Dragon Face!'

As the attendants ran in, the poor Taoist fell to his knees and beat his head upon the ground, the prospect of swift decapitation being rather more than his degree of imperturbability allowed for. But the Lord of Ten Thousand Years had recovered his equable temper and was more amused than indignant, for travelling in disguise had taught him the ways of ordinary men. Returning to his capital, he took the chastened Taoist in his train and enrolled him among the senior gardeners at the new Summer Palace he had just completed in the Western Hills, with special responsibility for the imperial peonies. Surely enough, the peonies next year were even lovelier than before and the Emperor, sending for his Taoist gardener, addressed him with that gracious blend of regal dignity and sincere deference that the Lord of Ten Thousand Years reserves for the Imperial

Tutors appointed to instruct him during the early years of his reign.

'Your Reverence has proved his point. We therefore desire to learn the art of inward-turned contemplation; for, greatly as it benefits the flowers, how much the more will Our mastering it benefit Our people!' Thus spake the Emperor and straightway appointed the Taoist abbot of a temple conveniently near the Summer Palace. Thereafter, His Majesty used to send for him in private and learn the secret art of contemplation from his lips.

Chapter 4

The Path of Faith and Compassion
Pure Land Practice

I had not been very long in China when, happening to visit the southern city of Weichou (Waichow), I hired a sampan to make a round of the lake-side temples there. The boat-girl, clad like most Cantonese boat-people in conical straw hat and black pyjama suit, stood in the stern, one foot before the other, strenuously plying the handles of the great wooden sweeps that crossed in front of her like giant scissors. *Eee-aw ee-aw* sang the sweeps in their wooden rowlocks – a pleasing soporific sound well suited to the sun-drenched scene. Blue water, pale blue sky flecked with fleecy clouds, vividly green hills rising abruptly as though hoping to be taken for mountains and, here and there along the shore-line, convoluted roofs peering out from thickets of bamboo and clumps of almond blossom. Presently we swung in towards a little temple, just a single shrine-hall of dark grey brick fronted by a slit-like courtyard of the kind known as 'sky-well' and a simple gatehouse, both buildings with green-tiled, upward-curving roofs supported on an elaborate arrangement of lacquered beams and pillars. As the sampan approached the temple steps, an elderly man with shaven head and loose monastic robe emerged and stood gazing fixedly towards us. When I stepped ashore, he welcomed me, palms pressed together before his chest in the Buddhist mode of greeting, murmuring the words 'Namu Omit'ou Fu' (Hail to the Buddha of Boundless Light). Repeating this formula in my turn, I bowed in deference to his age and standing, then followed him through the gatehouse where hung a horizontal board bearing the temple's name in gold caligraphy: P'U-MÊN T'ANG (Hall of Universal Entry). The sky-well was soon crossed and, stepping over the high door-sill, I found myself facing a black and gold altar of intricately carved wood furnished with the inevitable set of five ritual vessels, in this case fashioned of heavy pewter – an incense-burner flanked by great candlesticks with foot-high candles of crimson wax and, at each end, a vase containing sprays of almond-blossom. In the gloom behind the altar rose a statue of Kuanyin depicted as a graceful lady garbed in white and holding a slender vase of *amrita*, the nectar of wisdom. Her lovely face was lit by a faint smile, the eyes half closed like those of a nun rapt in blissful meditation.

Knowing what was customary in such circumstances, I took a handful of incense-sticks from a bundle lying on the altar, lit them at a glass-cased oil-lamp kept burning for the purpose and, standing with the scented smoke curling about me, intoned three times:

'Namu Ta-tz'û Ta-pei Kuanshihyin P'usa!' (Hail to the Merciful, Compassionate Bodhisattva, She-Who-Listens-to-the-Cries-of-the-World!). Then I kowtowed, thrice standing, kneeling and bowing my head to the floor in accordance with the ancient custom.

This done, I turned to the smiling monk, who led me through a moon-gate in one of the side-walls to an adjacent one-room dwelling, where a kettle simmered on a charcoal-stove ready for whatever guests might come. My host appeared to have few possessions beyond a narrow bed, some simple wooden furniture and a few utensils ranged on shelves in the closet-like recess that served both as kitchen and bathroom. Having put the questions with which it was customary in China to greet strangers – name, age, country, occupation and so forth – he told me he lived alone, having been deputed by the Abbot of the much larger temple to which this small one belonged to act as caretaker and see to the needs of visitors.

'It suits me well. As you know, there are much finer places of worship scattered around the lake; except on festival days, few people trouble to put in here, so my duties leave ample time for practice.'

As 'practice' might mean any kind of spiritual pursuit, I enquired what way he followed and he replied: 'Devotion to the Compassionate Bodhisattva Kuanyin. Praying for rebirth in that Pure Land called Potala where she resides – since I long to be trained as a Bodhisattva so that I, too, may share the task of liberating the countless beings endlessly revolving betwixt birth and death in samsara's bitter ocean – I recite her name many tens of thousands of times each day.'

Many tens of thousands of times each day? I glanced at him curiously. His wise and gentle mien proclaimed him a man of real spiritual attainment, one likely to be well advanced along the path to that high mystical goal which members of the Pure Land Sect, to which he obviously belonged, have in common with other Buddhists. Yet devotional recitation of a sacred formula and desire for rebirth in some sort of paradise seemed strangely at variance with Buddhist doctrine as I understood it, so much so that I had the temerity to remark:

'Your Reverence, I have often heard of this mode of cultivation and wish you would explain it. It is written that the Lord Buddha taught that this universe is by no means the creation of a supreme deity, that spiritual progress must depend not on pious aspiration but on the awakening of our own minds. I have read, too, that in speaking of the various orders of celestial beings, he affirmed that they also are wanderers in samsara subject to birth, growth, decay and death though their lives may be of immense duration, so that it is vain to turn to them for aid in winning Enlightenment. Have I understood correctly?'

Smiling, he bowed assent and I continued: 'Therefore, Your Reverence – forgive me if I seem discourteous – we Western students of the Way cannot help supposing that recitation of a sacred name and desire to be reborn in a heavenly realm are closer to the Christian way of praying for salvation than to the Buddha's injunctions to rely upon our own endeavours. We greatly admire his words: "Be lamps unto yourselves!" '

I felt rather ashamed of impugning the validity of his practice, for he was so clearly a man of much greater wisdom and spiritual attainment than I. I even fancied I could detect in him a quality of real holiness and it seemed audacious to address him in such terms, but he was not at all put out. Declining to debate the point, he answered quietly: 'Why be concerned with conceptual differences – mine, your own or others?' Concepts clutter the mind. Direct experience is the only way. Take a wooden-fish drum of the kind we use while chanting and, following its resonant notes, recite whatever sacred phrase you choose, withdrawing your mind from all external objects but the sound and remaining keenly attentive to what comes from within. In half an hour you will have made more progress towards understanding than could be expected from a month-long exposition of our doctrine.'

'Why the wooden-fish drum?'

'Percussion instruments of certain kinds are mysteriously effective. To say the least, better one rhythmical distraction than the hundred others that would leap into your mind if, being inexperienced, you sought to close all the gates of your senses simultaneously. Those hollow sounds, blending with the sacred words, make a music which – no, it is not something to be described. You should experience it for yourself. Unless you have something pressing to do before tomorrow, send your boat back to the city and tell the girl to return for you in the morning. You may sleep on my bed. I have somewhere else I can go on the rare occasions when I have a guest here.'

Attracted by his quiet smile and air of real holiness, I agreed at once. The boat-girl grinned happily when I handed her the full fare for a four-hour trip and promised to pay as much again for continuing it the next day. Unable to guess what the old monk had in store for me, I was content to await his pleasure. Watching the boat back away from the steps, he said simply: 'It is a joy to meet an Englishman who is a fellow-Buddhist. I hope this encounter will be memorable for us both, since it must result from some bond connecting us in a former life.'

Brewing fresh tea, we carried it out to his little lake-side garden where we could enjoy the breeze blowing up from the water. Idly we watched the colours of the landscape soften and presently some pleasure-junks put out from the further shore carrying, I was told, parties of well-to-do people from the city who would feast at sundown to the sound of music and perhaps enjoy the singing-girls in more ways than one. It was as though I had travelled back in time a hundred years to the China of days gone by. I enjoyed this sensation and, when a silence fell between us, had a curious notion that my companion was mentally communicating something of his inner peace.

'So that is the world', he observed, sweeping out his arm as if to present me with the beauty lying all about us. 'Where no attachments stains the mind, beauty is exalting. Hills, water, clouds and so forth fortunately make few demands. In admiring them, I am adoring the person of my patron Bodhisattva, Kuanyin.'

'In my country, Christians speak so about God. To them all nature is his holy and beloved creation. Is there not a parallel here?'

'I think not. Beauty and goodness represent Kuanyin to me, but equally they represent Wênshu Bodhisattva to his devotees and P'u-hsien Bodhisattva to certain others. They did not create the world, nor the ugliness, suffering and even horror that are sometimes masked by its beauty. Respectively they personify compassion, wisdom, goodness and one could say that they exist in the devotees' own minds.'

Puzzled by those last words, I just said: 'Tell me about Kuanyin.'

'That would take long', he answered. 'To different people she means different things, you see. An old folk story has it that she was a princess who took a vow of chastity, preferring a life devoted to the poor to spending her days keeping house for a rich husband. Her father, having betrothed her to a wealthy nobleman, was enraged by her refusal to wed and gave orders for her to be imprisoned in a small house within the palace gardens, crying: "Here you will stay until you promise to obey me!" Finding her obdurate day after day, he wrathfully

uttered some ferocious and ill-considered words which his
zealous attendants hastened to obey. In consequence the garden
house was set on fire. As the flames burst from its windows,
men and women rushed towards it crying: "Alas, alas for our
Princess!" But, before the blazing building collapsed, a snow-
white bird flew out from between the window-bars and soared
high into the sky, causing the onlookers to shout with joy.
Though their compassionate Princess would no longer live
among them, at least she had become a heavenly being and not
perished in the flames.

'There are many other stories of this kind pertaining, so it is
popularly supposed, to the different incarnations of that greatly
adored being. You will find her likeness everywhere. To the
Taoists and to common folk, she is a goddess, to us a Bodhisattva
or emanation of compassion. Most households contain a little
shrine where stands her image surrounded by pleasing objects
such as gleaming coral, delicate sea-shells or pearls perhaps. Her
shrines are scrupulously kept to symbolise her purity. A sure
refuge from disaster, sailors and fishermen pray to her in
moments of sea-peril. Though virginal, she is besought by
childless women to bestow the gift of sturdy, handsome sons.
You have surely heard of P'u-t'ou Shan (Potala Mountain),
the island off the Chekiang coast sacred to Kuanyin, where there
are many temples in her honour and a cave in which she is
revealed to the eyes of the faithful. Ordinary pilgrims see only
its rocky walls and sandy floor, whereas those to whom she is
pleased to manifest herself behold lotus flowers forming a living
carpet, in the midst of which one giant lotus unfolds its petals
and reveals Kuanyin gazing compassionately towards them.
Some, it is said, hear her voice. We need not doubt that people
who conceive of her in these simple ways – especially if they are
compassionate towards humans, animals and ghosts – do behold
her in such forms and enjoy her miraculous intervention in
their affairs.'

'And there are others, like Your Reverence, who see her
differently?'

'Oh yes, many others. To us, Kuanyin is no mere goddess but a glorious embodiment of the power of compassion. Within the great Void works a supremely powerful energy whence wisdom and compassion flow into every mind that is purified of dross and open to receive them. Formless and omnipresent, it produces emanations in as many forms as there are beings to conceive them. I have heard that, in India and Tibet, its compassion outflow is depicted in male form as Avalokitesvara Bodhisattva. Well, the name Kuanyin or Kuanshihyin bears the same meaning ("listening to the cries of the world") as that Sanskrit name, but we in China generally depict the Bodhisattva as a woman, which seems more appropriate to the quality of compassion. The invisible mind-energies proceeding from the Void take on, you understand, whatever forms our minds accord them. Since it is hard to feel devotion to abstract forces, our minds clothe them with forms we can visualise and love. In Cambodia, it is said, there are depictions of Kuanyin – or, rather – Avalokitesvara – as a horse. And why not? Bodhisattvas are manifested in whatever guise will best assist their liberating function, wearing the aspect of a king, a mendicant, a lovely girl, a mother, a horse, a fish. The invincible energy of wisdom-compassion is no myth; it is there for all to experience; what are illusory are the forms with which our minds endow it. To the serpent deities (*nagas*), Kuanyin doubtless appears in a form much like their own.

'As to my practice, it is thus. Visualising the Buddha-Compassion in the form of a pure and lovely being, I serve her by cultivating compassion myself, causing no wilful harm, helping beings as best I can, abstaining from the flesh of sentient creatures and withdrawing my mind from the passions and attachments that mar its purity. To me Kuanyin is also the water and the clouds and the mountains and the sky; the song of birds, the sound of water lapping and of the wind in the trees are her voice; the scents of flowers and fresh fruit are her fragrance, because all these things are worthy to be identified with the spirit of pure compassion. In truth all things are mind – not "my mind", "your mind" – just Mind. "I-ness", though real enough to our faulty perceptions, can be dismembered and caused to vanish by the power of mind. Hand, eye, body, preferences and aversions, tendencies, memories – in none of these resides an "I", which term in truth denotes merely a group of scattered, shifting components that change from moment to moment. Stripping these away in turn, one finds no "owner"; nothing remains of the seeming boundaries between mind and mind. Bodhisattvas are, like all things, mind-born – in essence the creation of eternal Mind, in form as various as the mental perceptions of the multitudes of beings.

'To return to the practice. Closing the doors of the senses, opening the mind to what lies within, one seeks to attain keen, objectless awareness. Since this is difficult, skilful means have to be employed. One such powerful means is one-pointed concentration upon the Bodhisattva-form chosen for devotion. A mind free from distraction because wholly concentrated upon the sound of the sacred name easily proceeds to objectless awareness. Ch'an followers who concentrate upon a *hua-t'ou* (*koan*) such as "Who reverences the Buddha?", meaning "Who is this so-called self?" achieve the same result. Essentially the two practices are the same. Deluded minds are like monkeys grasping at objects and throwing them down without discrimination. You must have noticed how thoughts come floating, whirling in when the doors of the senses are closed unskilfully; they are more pertinacious than flies round a wounded buffalo. Hence the need to concentrate upon just one object and then pass gently to the stage of entertaining no-thing. If that object is an exalted one, an embodiment of wisdom-compassion, so much the better; it prepares the mind for that which is found within when delusions cease, and it generates compassion that will stamp the meditator's thought and conduct at all times. Concentration upon the breath as it plays upon the tips of the nostrils also leads to one-pointedness and thence to objectless awareness, but that other gain is lost and thoughts of self-achievement may mar the result.

'Simple people may take recitation of the invocation to Kuanyin for a magical means to win the favour of a goddess. That does no harm. The practice, though begun at a different level, will not fail them. Indeed, illiterate folk often achieve objectless awareness more easily than others. Their minds are less cluttered.'

He smiled and sat studying my expression as though expecting me to argue that point, but I replied: 'Just so. One of my favourite stories is that of a Chinese peasant, somewhere in the border regions, who was enjoined by a Tibetan lama to recite the invocation associated with Avalokitesvara, OM MANI PADME HUM. The lama wrote it for him in Chinese and one of the peasant's barely literate friends, misreading the last syllable, assured him it had the same sound as the Chinese word for ox. Accordingly the peasant spent hours each day reciting "OM MANI PADME – ox"! The results were admirable, until someone pointed out his mistake and he corrected it. Thereafter he could achieve no worthwhile results at all and his lama, hearing of this after some time, advised him to go back to his old way of doing it, whereafter all went well. I suppose this man had a natural gift for meditation that worked well until his mind became cluttered with notions of a wrong way and a right way.'

He nodded and, after a moment's silence, I asked a question that for some time had been hovering in my mind: 'What follows when the point of objectless awareness is reached?'

Mastering his surprise at such naïvety, he answered: 'No one has ever found words to describe what occurs when conceptual thought is transcended. Words are inseparable from concepts. Take the taste of honey. You remember it as sweet and enjoyable; you will recognise it instantly when you eat honey again, but can you *describe* how it tastes? Saying it is sweet and yet different from syrup will not help someone who has never tasted it to know how it is. At best your question can be answered by poor analogies that are as likely as not to mislead people.'

Pausing to reflect awhile, he continued: 'When objectless awareness is attained, no trace remains of "I" and "other". The stream and its banks are one. The rain-drop has entered the pool. The flame has been swallowed by the fire. One cannot even say that bliss is there, for bliss and non-bliss are transcended, only that when one returns from that state it is with a memory of such bliss that nothing comparable exists beneath the boundless sky. Also there is mirth. The universe has lost its terrors. There is reverence in the heart and everything – puddles, kitchen shelves, a rusty pan, a common weed – is radiant with beauty.'

Greatly moved, I gazed at the moon lit lake, the bobbing lanterns of the pleasure-boats reminding me of fireflies. All of a sudden I felt hungry and my host, as though sensing this, left me alone while he busied himself preparing evening rice. Before long we were seated in his little dwelling dipping our chopsticks into some homely dishes concocted from beancurd, mushrooms and Tientsin cabbage. We had talked so long that he had omitted to perform the late afternoon rite that corresponds to vespers. This he now wished to remedy and I asked if I might join him.

Whether or not it was for my sake, the rite proved a very simple one. It consisted of an incense-offering chant, the recitation (accompanied on a wooden-fish drum) of a short work extolling Kuanyin's compassionate powers, some recitation of her sacred name and a closing chant invoking the blessing of tranquillity on all beings in 'the six states of existence'. Much of the time we stood facing the altar; but, during the recitation of the sacred name, we circumambulated the shrine, slowly at first, then faster as the old monk hastened the tempo of the hollow sounds produced by his wooden-fish drum. The slow and solemn BOK! BOK! BOK! gave place to such a rapid bok-bok-bok-bok, bok-bok-bok that I could hardly keep pace without breaking into a run. This was a ritual variant of the practice of reciting while seated with legs crossed in the meditation posture and could not be expected to produce the same profound effect; nevertheless, chanting 'Namu Kuan-shihyin P'usa' in time with the resonant voice of the wooden-fish brought a sense of mild exaltation. The flickering candle-light endowed the statue's lovely face with a hauntingly life-like quality; I could not help feeling that the compassionate Bodhisattva was watching me with some amusement.

The next morning, I assisted as best I could in a rite more elaborate and varied than the one described. It was over soon after sunrise and, an hour later, my sampan returned to bear me away to the other temples round the lake. When the time came to part, my host's expression was friendly and untroubled. I was sure he felt no sadness at being left without companions. Enjoyment free from attachment was after all an important part of his creed.

Devotees of the compassionate Kuanyin form one section of the Pure Land Sect (Ching T'u Tsung), which probably had more adherents in pre-communist China than any other form of Buddhism, just as (under the name Shin) it still has the biggest following among Japanese Buddhists, despite the apparent divergence of its doctrines from those generally accepted as the teaching of the Buddha. Western writers have gone so far as to describe the Pure Land Sect in such terms as 'a Far Eastern counterpart of Christianity in which nothing of Buddhism remains except the name'; others have ascribed a Nestorian origin to the sect or held that its doctrines derive from those of Central Asian devotees of the Sun Deity who resided at China's capital, Ch'ang An, during the T'ang dynasty. That so few of the Westerners who have recently espoused Buddhism have been attracted by that sect is doubtless due to its *apparent* similarity to the Christian religion which they have abandoned on the ground that Buddhism is more stimulating and acceptable to modern people, more consonant with prevailing scientific thought.

And yet? If such criticism is justified, it is strange that the

Pure Land Sect has had such a powerful impact upon the Far East. Moreover, Dr Daisetz Suzuki, that great proponent of Zen to whom the whole Zen movement in the West owes its being, declared in one of his books that many more people have attained realisation by Pure Land practice than by Zen. Indeed, the title of his very last work is: 'Shin Buddhism, Japan's Major Religious Contribution to the West' – *Shin* (Pure Land) Buddhism, not Zen! These considerations cannot be dismissed lightly.

Personally, I feel less concerned about reconciling Pure Land tenets with those of other forms of Buddhism than about showing convincingly that Pure Land cultivation is a valid (as well as comparatively simple) way of achieving the mystic's goal.

The central figure in Pure Land writings is Amitabha Buddha (Boundless Light), who is also reverenced in the form Amitayus Buddha (Boundless Life). The essential doctrine, a very poetic one, is as follows: The Amitayus Sutra states how the Buddha in the presence of a great concourse of celestial and terrestial beings, announced to the Elder Sariputra that, in the western part of the universe and lying beyond an infinite number of Buddha-realms is one known as Sukhavati, the Pure Land presided over by Amitayus Buddha, embodiment of Boundless Life and Light. Those who dwell there know no sorrow, only joy. Its lovely confines are filled with jewelled trees and there are seven jewelled pools where the 'water of eight merits' flows over golden sand, besides pagodas and pavilions wrought of gold, silver, crystal, pearl and other precious substances. From within the pools rise giant lotus flowers emitting rays of coloured light and an indescribably sweet fragrance. Heavenly music salutes the ears. Flowers rain down upon the golden earth and the songs of the birds there are sweetly melodious and holy. All these marvels have been called into being by Amitayus Buddha, whose person irradiates all quarters of that land with brilliant light; they result from his compassionate desire to liberate beings from aeon upon aeon of rebirth. All things there are conducive to this sacred purpose; the very songs of the birds and music of the breeze lead those who hear them to meditate continuously upon the Buddha's doctrine.

In another sutra it is explained that the Pure Land arose in response to the compassionate vow of Amitabha Buddha (who is identical with Amitayus) that, if any sentient being who yearned to enter such a realm concentrated on it whole-heartedly for as much as ten fleeting moments of thought and, in spite of that, did not succeed in being reborn there, he, Amitabha, would renounce the fruits of his own Enlighten-ment. According to the Amitayus Sutra, during the ten aeons since that vow was made, an inconceivable number of disciples have been attracted. including Arahants and Bodhisattvas. Whosoever hears that Buddha's name should yearn to be born in his Pure Land and dwell in that holy company. All good-hearted men and women, by repeating his sacred name from one to seven days with full concentration, can ensure that Ami-tayus will appear to them at the moment of death and welcome them to this Western Paradise. There they will dwell in happiness until they reach full Enlightenment, so hard to win in other circumstances.

Thus Amitabha's saving power is attributed to the stupen-dous force of the compassion felt by a pure being ready to renounce Ultimate Nirvana itself, sooner than leave other beings toiling and moiling in the ocean of sorrows. From this teaching has arisen the practice of daily reciting the sutras pertaining to the Pure Land and of meditating upon Amitabha's sacred name with unwavering concentration. Of very great interest is the fact that, whether devotees accept the teaching literally, as many of them do, or whether they regard it as an allegory conveying truths that cannot be communicated directly in words, the practice is equally efficacious in engendering the intuition that leads to mystical attainment and to the selfless compassion that springs from it. Those who take the Pure Land literally as a paradise to be entered from without often express their belief somewhat as follows:

F

'So great is the importance of reciting the sacred name with faith and concentration as often as we may that we even greet one another with the words "Namu Omit'ou Fu" (Hail to Amitabha Buddha) so as not to waste a moment on such trivialities as saying "Good morning" or "Goodbye", but no one really supposes that repetition of the name serves much purpose at moments when concentration is lacking. Gabbling the sacred name while dallying with thoughts of children, business or pretty girls is held to be an offence against purity of mind. Sometimes we are asked why we recite the sacred name so often, since the sutra clearly states that whole-hearted desire to be reborn in his realm though maintained for as little as ten fleeting thought moments, will assuredly bear fruit. Ah, but who can be sure that his concentration was unwavering even for that brief space of time? And how are we to retain purity of heart throughout our lives if the practice is abandoned? Now and then one hears it said that Amitabha's saving power is such that believers may live loosely and be wanting in compassion and yet attain the Pure Land by virtue of their faith. How dangerous is that doctrine! Who, having true faith in that pure being, would be tempted to live loosely or behave without compassion? Attaining unblemished purity of mind is a task never finished. Yet perfect concentration is possible only if the mind is pure, and the first requirement for purity of mind is purity of conduct. Therefore do we seek to live out our lives doing harm to none, eating only vegetables out of pity for sentient beings, cultivating compassionate thoughts and being ever generous to the needy. True, the merit thus acquired falls ten thousand yojanas short of the merit needed for achieving Enlightenment. Good works alone are of no avail, or would be so did we not cling to Amitabha's sacred vow; but, while we live in this world of dust, the way of purity and compassion is joyous. In days of old, there were many who, like Shakyamuni Buddha, attained Enlightenment after aeons of endeavour. Born into this age of decline, we are too burdened with ignorance and delusion to follow that exalted path; therefore do we seek rebirth in the Pure Land, that blissful realm where all things are conducive to a holy state of mind that will lead in good time to the attainment of Nirvana.'

On the face of it, the Pure Land doctrine – thus stated – does seem to have but little to do with Buddhism as generally understood and to be suited only to rather simple-minded people. It can reasonably be objected that Buddhism has always placed emphasis on self-purification from the three fires of anger, inordinate desire and delusion, on negation of ego-centred concepts by the devotee's own efforts, that the injunction against relying upon some deity for saving grace should also be applied to the Pure Land doctrine. How does faith in Amitabha differ in quality from faith in the saving power of some such a being as Jesus, which Buddhists reject as superstition? Then again, how can any man whose intellectual powers match the quality of his spiritual aspirations be moved by stories of jewelled lakes and trees, birds that preach the sacred Law and similar beguilements? Once, when I voiced such objections to a Pure Land *fa-shih* (*roshi*, accomplished teacher), he answered to the following effect:

'You have forgotten to add that research scholars have now cast doubt upon the authenticity of the whole body of Pure Land sutras. But never mind; their learned concern is pointless. And why? The Lord Shakyamuni Buddha, illustrious founder of our Buddhist religion, preached a subtle doctrine not easy to grasp by beings born in this degenerate age (*kaliyug*). Foreseeing how things would be, the Blessed One sanctioned the use of skilful means (*upaya*) to suit beings at each level of attainment. The members of our sect who accept descriptions of the Pure Land and of the way to attain it as literal truth lose nothing thereby, for that doctrine conveys a profound and holy truth in a manner that suits their understanding. Envisioning your destination as a city paved with gold will not hinder your getting there if you know the way. There are other members of our sect who perceive its doctrines to be clothed in poetic allegory. But all alike cultivate purity of mind and selfless

compassion, and there are many of both kinds who, concentrating on Amitabha Buddha's name, attain full realisation.
Do you suppose their realisation differs from that attained by
the followers of Ch'an doctrines? How could that be? Winning
to the Source of Wisdom and Compassion has nothing to do
with the name and form given to conceptions of that Source.
Nor are even the most simple monks and lay-folk as ignorant of
our doctrine's inner significance as you may suppose; for the
text of the evening rite performed in temples and monasteries
of every Buddhist sect throughout this land of China contains
the words: "Those who yearn to comprehend all the Buddhas
of the Triple World should know that the nature of the universe
is naught but mind"! Seen thus, that mental creation of the
compassionate Amitabha known as the Pure Land in no way
differs from the One Mind, which is also the Tao, the Void, the
Womb of the Tathagatas, that which alone exists forever –
formless, pure, infinite, eternal. To enjoy that mind-created
Pure Land, we too must create it in our minds, giving form to
the formless. Amitabha Buddha is no other than that Wisdom-
Compassion energy that stirs within all minds when stillness is
achieved and the error of self hood abandoned.

'Know, too, that the sutras describing his Pure Land speak
also of myriads of such Buddha-realms, for the power of mental
creation is so unlimited and this universe so boundless that our
poor world may be likened to just one grain of sand amidst all
the sands of the Ganges river. Infinite in extent is Mind and
there are as many Buddha-realms as there are minds enlightened
by wisdom and compassion to conceive them. As to our practice,
of the countless methods of withdrawing the mind from the
objects of the senses that the wisdom from within may flow
unimpeded, concentration upon a sacred formula is one of the
most effective. In the result, those who hold the Pure Land to
be a place that is entered from without perceive it so; those who
recognise it as an enlightened mental state experience it as pure
void. The sutras, in speaking of devotees of lower and higher
attainment, point to such categories of believers. The latter, as

you will readily understand, achieve full realisation more swiftly – but not more surely.

'Our Pure Land teachings are widely known as pertaining to "other-power" (*t'a-li*), whereas Ch'an teaching pertains to "self-power" (*tzû-li*); it is sheer delusion to suppose they differ. Mind knows no spatial bounds, no inside and outside, no self and other. If you hold that your mind and my mind can exist as entities apart from each other and apart from Mind itself, the efforts each of us makes will seem to pertain to self-power; when you recognise that your mind is empowered by Mind, you may speak of other-power; and when you reach the stage of seeing that your mind *is* Mind, you will cease all this gabble of self and other. So it is with the Pure Land. You may view it as "other", a place to be entered; or as "self", a place within you. Such conceptual distinctions are so much rubbish. The sooner you discard them, the wiser you will be.'

Whether this learned monk's exposition (couched in the simplest of words for my sake) helps to reconcile Pure Land teaching with Buddhist doctrine as a whole or not, the matter is one that decreases in importance as insight grows, for mystical attainment is a matter of direct experience having nothing to do with conceptual thought. That Chinese Buddhists saw no conflict between the doctrines of self- and other-power is evident from the fact that, even in Ch'an (Zen) monasteries, the morning and evening rites included recitation of the sacred name. The same monks sought 'other-power' inspiration in the shrine-hall and 'self-power' inspiration in the hall of meditation, their alternation being devised to save them from falling into pits of their own digging; for a single thought such as '*I* have attained such and such a stage' will send a meditator tumbling headlong as surely as an unlucky dice-throw sends the snakes-and-ladders player back to square 1. The erroneous concept, 'I', is very persistent in gaining admittance to the unguarded mind.

Most Chinese temples, whatever their sect, contained a statue of Amitabha; often there was a special hall in which his likeness

stood flanked by those of his principal emanations, the Bodhisattvas Ta Shih-chih and Kuanyin; and usually there was some
hall or shrine dedicated wholly to Kuanyin on account of her
wide popularity with lay devotees. The tendency of many Pure
Land adherents to make Kuanyin rather than Amitabha the
centre of their contemplation can, I think, be explained by a
natural association between the principle of compassion and
femininity. Among the deities of Egypt, Greece and the entire
ancient world of our history books, it was the mother goddess
who became predominant, as she remains today among many
sects of Hinduism; the Taoists long ago adopted Kuanyin as a
goddess; of the three main divisions of Christianity, both the
Orthodox and Catholic Churches accord special honour to the
Virgin Mary and there was a time when Wisdom (Sophia) was
virtually adored as a goddess by devotees within the Christian
fold. Similarly, many Buddhist schools and sects conceptualise
Wisdom-Compassion in female form – as Kuanyin or Tara.
This seems so entirely reasonable to me that I find it hard to
understand why the supreme deity (who must obviously
transcend any real male or female characteristics) is so often
portrayed as uncompromisingly male. It is more natural to
conceive of the source of all being in female guise. Laotzû speaks
of the Mother of the Universe (though not in an anthropomorphic sense) and 'womb of the universe' is a term that has
been used both by scientists and poets.

Though, understandably, some people may view Pure Land
doctrines as incompatible with Buddhism as a whole, a study of
Pure Land writings soon reveals that, metaphysically, they are
as much rooted in traditional Mahayana doctrine as those of any
other Mahayana Buddhist sect. This, however, is a point of
small importance in comparison with their real justification,
which is their efficacy in leading to realisation. It is their efficacy
which makes it not in the least surprising to discover that they
have close analogies with the doctrines and practices of many
other faiths. In this connection, one recalls: the invocations
employed by Sufi mystics, those extolled by Hindu adherents

of the way of *bhakti* ('Hare Krishna' and so forth) and the sacred formula that was used as a means of realisation by contemplatives within the Russian Orthodox Church. The manner in which such invocations are used scarcely differs from the employment by Pure Land followers of the sacred formulas 'Namu Omit'ou Fu' and 'Namu Kuanshihyin P'usa'. What is more, descriptions of the exalted experiences achieved in this or similar ways by mystics of different faiths reveal a striking similarity. Daisetz Suzuki, after a lifetime spent in studying and disseminating Zen doctrines, became so convinced of the wisdom of the Pure Land approach that he wrote in his last book: 'To rely on self-power is pride, and such pride is very difficult to uproot, as is belief in self-power.' However, his Pure Land belief was not the result of a very literal interpretation, for he also wrote: 'The Pure Land is experienced while here, and we are carrying it with us all the time. In fact the Pure Land is surrounding us everywhere. We become conscious of it, we recognise that Amida Buddha has come to help us after strivings have been experienced and exhausted.' (Amida is the Japanese form of Amitabha's name.)

Throughout the world and down the long corridors of history, there have always been seekers thirsting for the bliss of realisation. Their goal, the immaculate Tao, has been called by many names and the earlier stages of the way to it have differed, but not the goal itself. Where aspiration takes the form of yearning, the devotional path of faith and compassion is chosen; where it arises in a form no less compelling but more 'down-to-earth', a Zen-like path is preferred. Both these paths are intellect-transcending. They and other paths suited to various kinds and levels of perception, however much they differ at the outset, merge towards the end when conceptual thought is transcended. Sectarianism in the sense of vaunting one path and denigrating others is foreign to the Chinese tradition, so China's religious history in no way resembles the blood-stained annals of Christendom and Islam; many a staunch advocate of Ch'an (Zen) has paid moving tribute to Pure Land methods and vice versa. It is sad to find certain Western Buddhist writers speaking slightingly of Pure Land Buddhism, for at the very least its adherents have been lovable people steeped in the Buddhist virtues of tolerance and compassion, and realised mystics have not been few among them.

Much that was admirable in Chinese Buddhist traditions and institutions had its origin in Pure Land believers' concern for their fellow beings. I especially enjoyed visiting what were known as halls of virtue (*shan t'ang*). Resembling small nunneries, they often stood in pleasant rural environs within easy distance of a city. Many ladies used to go to them to spend a month or two in retirement from the world engaged in contemplative and devotional practices. These lay-institutions also served as centres for charitable endeavour and as homes of peaceful retirement for the elderly. Visitors were welcome and would be regaled by smiling old ladies with tea and sweetmeats or a delicious vegetarian meal. The precincts were always scrupulously kept and sometimes contained noteworthy examples of Buddhist art, but what I vividly remember is the serenity of those who dwelt there. Devotees of Amitabha or Kuanyin, they overflowed with kindness and gentle gaiety. Simple as they generally were, their whole presence was inspiring. Here was a Buddhist echo of the ancient Taoist philosophy that welcomed life and death with the same imperturbable tranquillity. The odours of incense and flowers that hung upon the air delightfully symbolised the Pure Land already established in their hearts.

Chapter 5

The Path of Learning
Mystically Directed Scholarship

It is widely accepted that learning and the cultivation of mystical intuition do not go well together. The one depends on conceptual thought; with the other, progress is seldom made until conceptual thought has been transcended. As one of my teachers used to say: 'If your mind is a vessel cluttered with objects of every colour, shape and size, how can you collect there the magical elixir – colourless, undifferentiated – that bestows experience of the Void? One coloured grain would mar the elixir's perfect purity.' Though he would go on to explain that the analogy had only limited application since form and void, being aspects of the same 'no-thing', are not two, he maintained that, below a high level of experience, they are perceived as two – the void aspect during one-pointed meditation, the multiform aspect at most other times, so that it made sense to speak of the mind's being cluttered with too much knowledge. And it is true enough that a highly intellectual mind often experiences great difficulty in achieving mystical experience.

The great sages of Taoism and Buddhism spoke with one voice in deploring the obstacles posed by too much learning. For example:

'Banish the wise! Away with the learned!'
'Those who know do not talk. Those who talk do not know!'
'To know and not be knowing is best.'
'The arrival of (specious) wisdom and intelligence generated great hypocrisy.'

'*Therefore the sage desires to be without desire, does not value what is hard to come by and learns (the wisdom of) not learning.*'

LAOTZŮ

'*You have heard of the knowledge that knows, but never of the knowledge that does not know. Look into the closed room, the empty chamber where brightness is born! Fortune and blessing gather where there is stillness.*'
'*Undo the mind, slough off the spirit!*'
'*The world values words and hands down books but, though the world values them, I do not think them worth valuing.*'

CHUANGTZŮ

'*Truth cannot be reached through name and form, nor understood by consciousness.*'

SÊNG CHAO

'*Directly pointing to the mind, my teaching is unique, not hindered by the teachings of the canons.*'

BODHIDHARMA

'*At a single stroke I forgot everything I'd known. Now there's no more need for cultivation.*'

HSIANG-YEN CHIH-HSIEN

'*Fa Ming enquired again: "The three divisions of the Mahayana canon are all the teaching of the Buddha. If we read them, recite them, have faith in what they teach, and act accordingly, how can we fail to come face to face with our own real nature?" Hui Hai replied: "All this is like a dog chasing after a lump of meat or a lion devouring a man. The three divisions of the Mahayana canon disclose the function of self-nature – reading and reciting them are mere phenomena arising from that nature."*'

HUI HAI

'*Only renounce the error of intellectual or conceptual thought-processes and your nature will exist in its pristine purity.*'

'Just spread out a net
For reclining quite flat.
When thought's tied to a bed
Like a sick man grown worse,
All karma will cease
And all fancies disperse
– THAT's what is meant by Bodhi!'

HUANG PO

Pietists who hold that scriptural study is the foundation of all goodness and scholars who maintain that learning is the road to wisdom, like those who expect salvation from good works, are generally not mystically inclined. Nevertheless, in China there have been Buddhist monks and laymen who set much store by scholarship, cherishing the belief that profound knowledge of Mahayana principles, though not an end in itself, is a valuable preparation for mystical experience. The essential difference between these scholar-mystics on the one hand and the icono-clastic anti-scholars among Taoists and Ch'an (Zen) followers on the other resulted from their different ways of regarding the relationship of learning to intuitive progress. The scholars believed that a firm basis for mystical intuition is to be found in intellectual understanding of such difficult concepts as Void-ness *(Sunyata)*, the mutual penetration of the two levels of truth (absolute and relative), the illusory nature of the ego, the identity of opposites and so forth. To the Taoists and Ch'an (Zen) followers, on the contrary, all this seemed not merely a pointless waste of time, but the sheerest folly, since forming *concepts* of the Great Mystery is the surest way to hinder intuitive realisation.

Scholar-mystics were to be found principally among the adherents of three sects – T'ien T'ai (called after a mountain of that name), Hua Yen (a name taken from that of an important sutra) and Wei Shih (meaning 'Nothing But Consciousness', hence 'Pure Consciousness'). In my day, these sects only barely existed as separate entities, but their doctrines were still studied by individual monks belonging to other sects and also by learned laymen. Having received no direct teaching from adherents of those doctrines, I can give no more than a bald account of them, yet it would not do to omit them altogether from a work on Chinese mysticism.

The T'ien T'ai Sect (Japanese, Tendai) was in many respects close to Ch'an (Zen) Buddhism and will be mentioned more fully in connection with the path of meditation. Its fourth patriarch, Chih K'ai (sixth century A.D.) was himself a Ch'an adept, but he opposed that sect's insistence on discarding book-learning and rejecting externals that seemed to him to have importance. It was he who gave shape to the distinctive T'ien T'ai doctrines. Besides writing many treatises, he made a profound study of the Mahayana canon, especially the works of Nagarjuna and the sutra known as The Lotus of the True Law. His studies convinced him that there is no fundamental antagonism between the teachings of the various Mahayana sects, nor between Mahayana and Theravadin Buddhism, their varied doctrines having been separately propounded to suit disciples at different levels of understanding. The sutras, or sermons of the Buddha, he divided into four categories, classifying them as having been delivered over five different periods of the Buddha's lifetime. His careful scholarship was in line with the Confucian tradition in which all highly educated men in those days had been reared; his doctrines have always had a special appeal for the more erudite among Chinese Buddhists, some of whom have propounded the view that there is no essential difference between the scholarly and intuitive approaches to realisation. One such scholar offered me the following analogy: A doctor in making a diagnosis generally relies not only upon observation, but also (especially if he is a traditional-style Chinese physician) upon a high degree of intuition. In order to diagnose correctly and rightly interpret his intuition, he must first have studied medicine for many years. Similarly, though the attainment of mystical realisation is an intuitive process requiring the relinquishment of conceptual thought, people would not wish or know how best to do that, unless previously instructed. Since mind-to-mind transmission requires exceptional powers, the instruction must in most cases be oral, written or both, involving conceptual thought on the part of both teacher and pupil. Thus learning has its place as a usually indispensable support to the attainment of intuition. There is much to be said for this view. For example, the delight with which I have viewed the progress of Ch'an (Zen) in the West has sometimes been tempered with dismay. Too many people, seizing blindly upon the phrase 'a doctrine without words' have plunged into meditative practice with insufficient preparation. Some of their writings are either disappointingly superficial or dangerously misleading. There is a Chinese saying that, though wisdom *(prajna)* is the highest goal, both discipline and knowledge are essential to its attainment.

The sutra from which the Hua Yen Sect (Japanese, Kegon) derives its name is said to have been preached by the Buddha two weeks after his Enlightenment to an audience of Bodhisattvas, etc., no humans being present. Recognising that this doctrine was beyond human comprehension, the Buddha, it is said, subsequently delivered other discourses better suited to their understanding. Meanwhile the sutra was hidden in an iron tower that was subsequently opened by Nagarjuna with the help of seven grains of mustard seed. Within the tower were found three versions, one consisting of innumerable stanzas, one of medium length and one composed of a mere hundred thousand stanzas, of which only the last was henceforth used, the others being too difficult to grasp. There are scholars who declare this Hua Yen Sutra to be a comparatively late composition inspired by the doctrines of the Yogacarya School that was once very prominent in Indian Buddhism. However that may be, it is concerned with the relativity of phenomena and, above all with the nature of the Ultimate – the Buddha-realm of Infinity. Inspired by this sutra, the founders of the Hua Yen Sect, such as Tu Shun, Chih Yen and Fa Tsang (all seventh century A.D.), produced a philosophy which harmonises all the great Mahayana teachings. The Hua Yen concepts and the meditations to which they lead have an awe-inspiring grandeur. Perhaps no other system of human thought has come so near to capturing in words the vastness and multidimensional nature of Infinity, known to the sect's adherents as Universal Mind and likened to a 'vast Ocean Mirror'. Reading or meditating upon facets of this majestic doctrine, one may experience the giddiness that sometimes comes from looking down upon a widespread panorama from the peak of a high mountain. With this sect, study of the written word becomes more than preparation for intuitive realisation; the imagery of the Hua Yen Sutra is so tremendous that it may plunge one into a sudden and terrifying perception of truths that go far beyond what the words themselves convey. Here are two passages translated by Garma C. C. Chang which, though they lack the subtlety and depth of many of the other passages he has rendered into English, convey something of the sheer size and mystery of the universe as conceived by Mahayana Buddhists:

'Oh sons of the Buddha! If a man pulverises millions and billions of Buddhas' universes (each consisting of a thousand million solar systems) and reduces them to dust-motes, each of which represents another universe, and again he pulverises these universes and holds the total number of dust-motes acquired thereby in his left hand and walks eastward; and after passing over the same vast number of universes, he then drops one dust-mote and continues walking eastward, and each time he passes over the same number of universes, he drops another dust-mote until he exhausts all that he held in his hand; if he then walks south, north and west in the four directions and upward and downward, dropping dust-motes as before, O, Pao Shou, what do you think? The total space in the ten directions of all these universes touched or untouched by his dust-motes, is this space of a Buddha-land not vast, broad and beyond comprehension?'

'Unfathomable are the countless worlds
In the totality of universes.

Many worlds are new or are decaying,
While many others cease to be.
Like leaves in a forest,
Some flourish others fall . . .
As different seeds give birth to different fruits,
Or magicians project conjurations with their spells,
So sentient beings by the power of (collective) karma
Make various world-systems that are incomprehensible.'

The three essential Hua Yen doctrines are those of the Void, Mind Only and Totality. The first is basic to any Mahayana work and helps in understanding many Taoist works as well; all things from world galaxies down to our illusory egos must be viewed as perfectly void at the level of absolute truth, their formless state nevertheless existing simultaneously with the transitory forms that are perceived at the level of relative truth. The doctrine of Mind Only is one also propounded (though with less lucidity) by the Ch'an (Zen) Sect. The doctrine of Totality reveals that all realms or modes of existence, however contradictory they seem, co-exist with one another and inter-penetrate without the least obstruction. To acquaint the Empress Wu with the significance of this last doctrine, the Master Fa Tsang caused a Buddha-image to be placed in a chamber of which ceiling, floor and walls were all composed of mirrors. Naturally, each of those mirrors reflected not only the central Buddha-image, but its reflections in all the other mirrors and the other mirrors themselves, thus hinting at the marvellous and effortless penetration of all realms. Next, he produced from his sleeve a small crystal ball in which all this was, of course, reflected, demonstrating that the principle of non-obstruction has no limits, since the small contains the great just as harmoniously as the great contains the small.

The profundity of Hua Yen philosophy can by no means be conveyed in a few words. Suffice to say that, though Hua Yen adherents naturally practised meditation, it was of a kind that required a good grounding in tenets too subtle to have much popular appeal. Therefore Hua Yen teachings were prized by scholars and by experienced meditators belonging to other sects, who found in their splendid imagery confirmation of their own intuitive experiences and stimulation to ever higher modes of understanding.

Of the Wei Shih Tsung or Pure Consciousness Sect I know very little except that its exponents were more often scholars than mystics. Its teachings were introduced into China by the famous monk and pilgrim, Hsüan Tsang (seventh century A.D.), who was the translator (or, as some say, the author) of the very important Treatise on Achieving Pure Consciousness. The sect seems never to have been widespread; but, during the present century, interest in its doctrines was revived, especially in circles like those of the scholar-monk T'ai Hsü, who sought correspondences between Buddhism and modern science. Unlike most other Mahayana sects, Wei Shih belongs to what is called the *fa-hsiang (dharmalaksana)* school of thought sometimes equated with philosophic realism, though 'modified idealism' would be a better term for it since it emphatically lays down that matter is composed of consciousness. It differs from idealism as normally understood in postulating entities known as 'seeds of consciousness' which are infinitely varied in kind, those stored within our minds being responsible for our varied karma. It is difficult to conceive of consciousness as consisting of these 'monads' and I shall not presume to interpret the meaning. In one sense, the doctrine fits in with a widely held Buddhist concept that the realm of form consists of series of innumerable impulses (*dharmas*) which come and go in a flash. Now *that* is a doctrine which I do understand at least to a limited extent. On the only occasion when I ventured to try one of the hallucigens and was rewarded by the experience of an agonising tension – far worse than physical pain – I did what I had been taught to do in dire extremities with the result that I was transported to a state of bliss in which I came face to face with several realities that I had formerly understood and accepted only at the intellectual level. Besides comprehending with perfect (though, alas, temporary) clarity how things may simultaneously be one and many, I experienced consciousness as the rise and fall of an infinite number of successive impulses that emerged and vanished like quickly bursting bubbles. But these quickly vanishing *dharmas* can surely not be equated with the Wei Shih seeds of consciousness, for it is impossible to conceive of the former as being '*stored* in the mind'.

Far from being mystics as that term is ordinarily understood, Wei Shih adherents sought to achieve realisation of reality as consisting of pure consciousness by a careful investigation of the specific characteristics of phenomena. Where they saw eye to eye with Mahayana Buddhists in general, and incidentally with Taoists, was in admitting no fundamental difference between the universal and the individual. What was specific to the Wei Shih Sect was the doctrine that consciousness can be divided into eight categories, six of which correspond to the perceptions of the five senses and of the intellect, while the seventh (discrimination) forms a link between those six and the eighth which, known as *ālaya-vijñāna*, is the storehouse from which proceed the seeds of consciousness – the root of consciousness and, indeed, original consciousness itself.

The path of learning impinges on the mystic's path in cases where some passage or other in a sacred text produces in one who reads or hears it a sudden illumination that is wholly intuitive and transports him far beyond the realm of words and concepts. The most famous case of this in the history of Chinese Buddhism is that of Hui Nêng, Sixth Patriarch of the Ch'an Sect, who is said to have reached full realisation when, returning from selling firewood, he happened to overhear someone reciting the Diamond Sutra. As this anecdote is already very well known, I offer another of rather similar nature that was told me by an old monk I encountered on Mount Omei during World War Two. It is a good example of mystical realisation obtained directly by one who followed the path of learning, as opposed to the employment of learning merely as a preparation for mystical endeavour. Before relating it, I may

G

add that I can well believe in such startling possibilities. I am convinced that, if one were to read the Hua Yen Sutra – especially if it were by candlelight in some lonely place – and ponder its awe-inspiring imagery, a profound mystical experience might burst upon one unawares! This is what the old monk told me:

'There dwelt in a small and dilapidated temple not far from Wênchou, where I was born, a monk known as Chih Tsang who was an ardent seeker of the Way. In his youth he had been a Confucian and had passed the first round of civil service examinations; but, full of disillusion with the world of dust, he had thrown up his studies, rejected the offer of a junior appointment and taken to the life of a hermit monk. When he first came to that little temple, it was to serve and cherish his teacher, a venerable monk known far and wide for his penetration of the Hua Yen doctrine; but the old man soon afterwards passed away and Chih Tsang, too modest to take a disciple of his own, thenceforth lived in solitude. People from the neighbouring village, admiring his piety and hoping to win merit by supporting him, brought him offerings of rice, oil and vegetables, or occasionally cloth for garments, but seldom intruded on his privacy.

'Owing to his habit of looking at everything from a scholar's point of view, Chih Tsang made little progress towards winning insight and presently abandoned meditation; yet, reflecting how hard it is to attain rebirth as a human being and, even then, to be born into a land where the doctrine of the Buddha is proclaimed, he longed to achieve some degree of realisation in this very life. To that end, he read and reread the Hua Yen Sutra and many learned treatises purporting to expound its inner meaning, committing whole chapters to memory in the hope that realisation would flower in his mind. As a man of education, he found it easy to understand the philosophical aspects of the Hua Yen teaching, so much so that, had he chosen the life of a *fa-shih* (accomplished preacher), he would doubtless have had disciples in plenty and achieved a certain empty fame, but that was not his way. Kneeling before the Buddha morning and evening, he used to pray: "Compassionate Buddha, do not let me take rebirth as an animal or hungry ghost, nor even as a human born in a land where the Buddha Dharma is not preached. I am thirsty for Enlightenment, not from a longing for Nirvana's peace, but that I may assist in the holy task of ferrying sentient beings across life's bitter ocean. In meditation, my mind becomes irritable and wayward thoughts come swarming like a host of noxious insects; whereas, when I recite the Hua Yen Sutra, my mind becomes clear and I rejoice for a time in the subtlety of my understanding. But, Compassionate One, you have taught that understanding without direct perception is nothing but a source of pride and a piling up of mounds of refuse. Therefore help me. Even a small ray of direct perception would be enough to fill me with joy."

'One night, Chih Tsang, sitting late over his studies, came to a well known passage in the Hua Yen Sutra which states that the Buddha and sentient beings are one since, in reality, nothing exists but Mind. Pondering this saying, as he had done many times before, he tried in vain to perceive his identity with all other beings. Intellectually, that was possible, but in his heart of hearts he could not *feel* it was so. Suddenly there came the sound of fleet footsteps and a banging on the door, which opened to admit a young man clad in tattered silken garments who stank of wine. This youth, aware that Sons of the Buddha (as Buddhist believers are sometimes called) were by nature compassionate, did not blush to admit that the magistrate's runners were hard upon his heels because he had killed his elder brother during the course of a drunken brawl in the brothel quarter of the district capital lying some miles to the north. Having gabbled out this shameful story, he begged the monk to hide him until the pursuit died down.

'As a one-time Confucian, Chih Tsang felt a horror of this young man, the slaying of an elder brother being only slightly less heinous than parricide according to the Confucian code.

His first thought was that here was a worthless scamp who fully deserved the dire penalty that the law inflicted in such cases; but, even as he opened his mouth to shout to the fellow to be gone, he had a vision of himself kneeling in the centre of the execution ground and experienced in full the sensation of waiting for the headsman's sword to fall. He recovered from this momentary trance filled with an overwhelming compassion that puzzled him by its vehemence. It was as though he were a mother watching her only son being sucked into a whirlpool! Swiftly he conducted the young man to a safe hiding-place in a press where kneeling-cushions for the temple ceremonies were stored, then blew out his candle and hurried to bed so that, when the lictors burst in upon him, he seemed to have been roused from sleep and to know nothing of the fugitive. Thus the wrong-doer was saved.

'Thereafter, whenever Chih Tsang saw a fellow being in trouble, though it might be just a small animal or insect, he experienced the same compelling urge to save it at whatever cost to himself and would have been ready to give his life to ease its pain. Useless to tell himself that such an agony of pity was excessive. Presently he came to recognise that things had fallen out in accordance with his yearning; the words of the sutra had so illumined his mind that, without passing through the ten stages of the path, he had attained to the compassion of a Bodhisattva! Hurrying to his long disused meditation cushion, he folded his legs and instantly attained objectless awareness. Thenceforth, until his death at a ripe old age, he ceased reciting and studying the sutras, spending all his days in meditation and attaining realisation upon realisation; for his mind had been transformed in a flash from that of an ignorant being (*fanfu*) into pure *Bodhicitta* (mind as the essence of Wisdom and Compassion).'

There are many similar stories of devotees who attained realisation by a flash of wisdom ignited by sudden apprehension of the hidden meaning of some passage in the sutras, but I know of no account of Enlightenment's occuring wholly as the cumulative result of sacred learning. At most one can say that learning may sometimes prepare the ground for an instantaneous intuitive experience.

Chapter 6

The Path of Meditation
Pure Land, T'ien T'ai, Ch'an (Zen) and Esoteric Methods

The word 'meditation' is widely current in the world today with just the meaning it has here – a general term covering all kinds of mental yoga aimed at stillness, pacification of thought, investigation of the true nature of being and attainment of that high mystical experience wherein the individual's mind is united with Mind, the Source of Being. 'Meditation' is an unsatisfactory term, for in every-day language it means 'thinking about something', which is exactly what the yogic meditator must not do, since the aim is to *transcend* conceptual thought. Even in Chinese it is difficult to find one term that covers all the various contemplative practices and many Chinese just call it *ta-tsuo* – sitting. This would be as good a term as any, were it not that meditation teachers are forever asserting that the practice can be performed 'standing, walking, sitting or lying'. So, instead of discussing terms and definitions, it will be better to begin with a story that illustrates what actually happens.

Shutting the Gate
In pre-communist China and Tibet, there were many large monasteries famed for the strictness of their régimes and the excellence of their meditation practice, but I found it easier to come into contact with dedicated contemplatives in small, remotely situated temples where the monks could meditate in their own way unhampered by time-tables and special rules. Some of the contemplative monks I met were eccentrics, like

one I remember who lived in a cave subsisting on grass and candles; he had once been in prison on the improbable charge of being a communist agent and had actually enjoyed living in that insanitary, vermin-ridden place where the food was barely enough to sustain life, for, as he said: 'I was left to meditate in peace, undisturbed by pious pilgrims with tiresome questions.' But the meditator who made the most powerful impression on me was one who lived in a rustic temple in the central part of Shantung province. Approached by a narrow path through millet-fields that resembled at that season a wilderness of mud-baked yellow earth, it nestled among low, almost treeless hills. Though its shrine-hall still bore traces of former magnificence, the rest consisted of more ordinary buildings of yellow mud-brick, hardly better than the dwellings of poor peasants, but the atmosphere of holiness was unmistakable, being due to rather more than the fragrance of incense that hung upon the air.

Within this temple dwelt three people – an elderly monk in patched grey robes, a novice who was but a lad and another monk who usually remained invisible to visitors. The two who came out to greet me on my arrival seemed disconcerted by the sight of an 'Ocean Devil' carrying luggage and presumably expecting to be invited to pass the night there, but my knowing how to speak Chinese and how a lay-guest should conduct himself soon put them at their ease and they became very friendly. There was nothing at hand for supper but coarse millet gruel; so, rather than seem inhospitable, they broke the monastic rule enjoining strict vegetarian diet by procuring some boiled eggs from a neighbour, which they served to me in a heavy soy-sauce. For themselves they had no relish but a few leaves of salted cabbage. Attacking the gruel with an appetite sharpened by my journey, I delighted them by swallowing bowlful after bowlful as though oblivious of its coarseness; it was this, I am sure, that won them over to talk and laugh without the least hint of constraint. Though very poor, they were determined to do their best for me and the novice scoured the village in search of tea-leaves of fairly good quality.

When I asked about their régime, they told me it was their habit to go to bed very early, rise at midnight and perform a special rite that lasted until it was time for the morning ritual that takes place in almost all Chinese Buddhist temples around dawn. The special rite consisted of facing the altar and intoning a musical invocation to Amitabha Buddha, taking it in turns to kneel head to the ground, so that as the one sank to his knees the other would rise, their chanting never ceasing.

'And you do that *every* night? I asked. 'I thought it was done only occasionally as a kind of penance.'

'We do it for the Venerable Shêng Tsang', explained the elderly monk. 'Last month he fell ill and we vowed to take his evil karma upon ourselves in this way, with the result that he has now recovered.'

'The Venerable Shêng Tsang?'

'Yes, our Chief Monk. We shall take you to see him tomorrow. He came here from one of the great meditation centres in Anhui. He has "shut the gate" (*pi kuan*) for three years and there are still some months to go. He seldom breaks silence, but may do so for a visitor from so very far away.'

The term loosely translated 'shut the gate' refers to the practice of remaining in seclusion behind a sealed door for a number of years, the better to conduct uninterrupted meditation. Once of twice a day, food is passed in and slops removed through a small window, but it is rare for the adept to speak to those who perform this service.

That night I slept like a log, to be wakened at dawn by the booming of the huge drum that marks the beginning of the morning ritual. After a breakfast of tea and ô-t'ou (coarse *kaoliang* rolls that are very palatable when fresh), I was taken to a building consisting of a store-room and a much smaller chamber, the door of which was pasted over with paper stamped with a great red seal, like those seen in the corners of Chinese paintings but many times larger. A square hole had been cut into the mud-brick wall and a lattice with translucent window-paper inserted. Standing close to the lattice, the novice shouted: 'Venerable, a devil-man has come.' He was but a country bumpkin and intended no rudeness, not knowing how else to call me; it was something I had long ago got used to and never resented unless the words were said by someone sufficiently educated to know better, but that rarely happened.

'Eh? Eh?' came a voice. 'Little Bean-Child, you must learn not to disturb me with such trifles. Recite the Mantra of Great Compassion with true fervour and the creature will vanish.'

The novice looked uncomfortable, but grinned when he saw me laughing. 'I am an Englishman', I cried. 'A Buddhist. I have come to pay my respects to the great monk.'

'Ha!' The lattice was lifted down bodily from inside, revealing a middle-aged monk seated cross-legged on a couch a foot or so from the aperture in the wall. As was fitting, I made three prostrations, during which the novice so oddly called Bean-Child brought me a chair. The hermit, having never before heard of a Western Buddhist, showed a lively curiosity about my circumstances and it was some time before I could get him to talk about himself. It did not matter. Perhaps because he had few visitors, he showed no disposition to put an end to the audience. Learning that he had not only remained shut up in that room for two and a half years but had previously spent two three-year periods in similar solitude, I questioned him eagerly about his practice.

A native of Shantung belonging to a relatively well-to-do family, the Venerable Shêng Tsang had 'left home' at the age of eighteen, passed a two-year novitiate in the small temple where his teacher resided and then received ordination at the Chieh T'ai Szû Monastery near Peking. Thereafter he had gone to live in a large, strictly conducted monastery in central China which specialized in meditation practice. Starting with the *huat'ou* (*koan*) practice of the Ch'an Sect, he had progressed to the more elaborate T'ien T'ai method.* For a couple of years, he had held the post of Preceptor, instructing the younger monks in meditational techniques, but had found this duty

* Shortly to be explained.

uncongenial because distracting. So, twelve years earlier, he had moved to the rustic temple where I found him. During each three-year period of seclusion, he had followed an identical régime; to me it seemed terribly demanding, but he looked well enough and his only illness had been due to an infection that had spread in the locality. Certainly he was thin and rather pallid, but that was the least to be expected in the circumstances and could largely be accounted for by the poor diet in that temple. His eyes were preternaturally bright and he impressed me as being mentally energetic and alert. Though not especially good-looking, he wore an air of stillness and simplicity – an air I was one day to recognise as characteristic of advanced contemplatives. The régime he described consisted of what must have amounted to some sixteen hours a day of meditation, either sitting cross-legged or walking slowly up and down his little cell, during which time, so he assured me, his thoughts never wandered. For four hours every night and for one hour in the afternoon, he slept sitting in a cross-legged position, never lying down even for a moment unless ill. Allowing perhaps half an hour in all for his two simple meals, that left two and a half hours each day; these were spent either in reading and rereading the dozen or so volumes of sutras and other sacred writings he had with him, or else in reciting a devotional formula to the Bodhisattva Manjusri, embodiment of the Buddha Wisdom, which runs: 'Namo Ta-chih Wên-shu-sê-li P'u-sa Mo-ho-sa!' (Hail to the Supremely Wise Manjusri Bodhisattva Mahasattva!).

When I remarked that I should find even three days of such practice unbearably rigorous, he laughed heartily.

'No, no. Only beginners find it so. Sleep while sitting up soon comes with practice. True, never allowing the mind to rove idly is impossible at first, but with time everything becomes easy. It is just a matter of habit. Sustained meditation, though fatiguing to beginners, is restful to those accustomed to it. Blissful, too! No strain. The mind not permitted to dwell on anything becomes like a mirror that reflects the passing scene, grasping at nothing, clinging to nothing. In earlier years, I divided my time between three kinds of meditation – first, *samadhi* (*ting*) achieved by resting the mind on a single object which presently vanishes amidst the ecstacy of objectless awareness; second, penetration of the voidness of opposites and thus of the voidness of the self; third, contemplation of the arising and passing away of thoughts in the mind. Now I make no such distinctions. Except when reading, reciting or sleeping, I dwell all day long in objectless awareness. To recall me when it is time for my morning and evening recitation, one of the others goes to the shrine-hall next door and strikes the sounding-bowl; otherwise I should not know, for all sense of time departs.'

When he fell silent, I prostrated myself and left, feeling dizzy at the thought of holding the mind in a state of objectless awareness for many hours at a time. Even now, I cannot imagine how it must be to retain alertness and yet hold no object in mind for more than a brief period.

Theoretically meditation is accepted as the very core of Buddhist practice, as the sole means for eliminating those erroneous perceptions which lead to 'unskilful deeds of body, speech and mind' whereby endless chains of karmic action are set in train; insight into the true nature of being requires a revolution of mind scarcely attainable by other means. In practice, many Buddhists find it difficult and rely on securing a more propitious rebirth by behaving with reasonable self-restraint and generosity to others; but, unless one postulates a father-deity able to reward and punish, it must be obvious that every being is responsible for his own progress, that there can be no 'getting by' on the ground that he has done his best to behave as he should. Therefore meditation leading to illumination of mind is essential in a Buddhist context; even the Pure Land style recitation of a sacred formula requires supreme concentration to be effective.

The traditional description of illumination is that it consists of experiencing the voidness of all entities, including the supposed 'self' – voidness in the sense that they are but transient and exist only in mutual dependence on everything else, thus being devoid of own-being. This may seem a chilly sort of goal to aim for, but innumerable adepts have testified to the bliss of attaining it; it is an experience not of diminution, but of sudden and glorious magnification, for the tiny 'individual mind' rejoices in sudden recognition of its identity with infinite Mind itself.

Chinese and Tibetan techniques of meditation are too numerous to list comprehensively, although some Chinese Masters reduce all of them to two categories – *ting* (one-pointedness) and *kuan* (reflective contemplation). I would prefer to divide them into six main categories, as follows:

1. Pure Land type meditation which, whether the Pure Land is initially taken literally to be a place – a kind of paradise, or whether it is recognised as the devotee's own mind in the purified form that frees him from the concept of mind as being 'his own', leads ultimately to the same result.

2. Visualisations of tantric type in which qualities of the devotee's own mind and the transcendent qualities of Mind are initially perceived in the form of beings, benign and wrathful, as a special technique for achieving direct awareness of mind's true nature.

3. Reflective contemplation: (*a*) to arouse revulsion against samsaric life's inherent unsatisfactoriness and thus eliminate passion and inordinate desire; (*b*) to prepare for the experience of voidness by mentally stripping objects of successive layers of self-ness until it is recognised that there is nothing to them that is not transient and dependent; (*c*) to deepen compassion by reviewing the sorrows of others individually and in the mass with pity, their joys with sympathetic gladness, their strengths and weaknesses with love, and all sentient beings with impartial equanimity.

4. Watching the mind, that is observing wayward thoughts as

they arise and fade, while remaining free from attachment to them and tranquilly letting them go.

5. Achieving objectless awareness leading to inner stillness, to 'resting in the Tao', for which there are several techniques such as concentration upon a mantra, or upon the play of breath at the tips of the nostrils, or upon one of the body's psychic centres, etc., or directly setting out to achieve one-pointedness.

6. Investigation into the nature of the 'self', sometimes by use of a *hua-t'ou* (*koan*) of which the essential meaning in many cases is 'Who really am I?', sometimes by other means.

Mere intellectual understanding is never the aim. There must be conscious effort at first; then, as it were, something (or nothing) begins to take over and the meditation becomes wholly passive. Effort in the sense of straining is absolutely to be avoided. Higher and higher states of consciousness are reached, of a kind that cannot even be guessed from studying a list of methods, nor ever described except obliquely by means of analogy. For here the Great Mystery of which Laotzû spoke is encountered face to face.

Within the Ch'an (Zen) Sect there has been much argument as to whether realisation of 'original being' is sudden or gradual. Clearly it is both. The expansion and deepening of consciousness is a gradual process that cannot often be dispensed with, but the attainment of full awareness whereafter no shadow of delusion remains takes place in a flash. It is as though hitherto one has been observing the fragments of a glass painting of the universe arranging themselves in endless transformations like those seen in a kaleidoscope – when, all of a sudden, everything clicks into place and the universe is intuitively experienced as it really is.

An important point insisted upon by almost all meditation teachers is that meditation should be combined with devotional practice. In the West, there are people who, revolting against the shackles of traditional religion, have come to have a high regard for meditation but shun religious rites as mere trappings suited only to the ignorant. In the East, Mahayana (including Zen) and Theravada Buddhists are at one in holding that to meditate but refrain from bowing down in salutation to the Triple Gem (the Buddha, the Doctrine and the Order), burning incense and performing similar devotional rites, is wrong and dangerous. As one of my Tibetan teachers put it: 'Meditation aims at transcending the notion of "I". If the meditator does not humble himself before his lama and the Triple Gem, he will be visited by such reflections as: "I have made this progress. I have attained such and such a mental state." No sooner does such an unskilful thought flash into his mind than all his progress is undone; the "I" instead of being diminished rejoices in its imaginary achievement.'

Surely that must be so, for what is the point of meditation other than to realise identity with the Greater-than-I, which is the Tao, the Buddha Mind, the Godhead – call it what one will? Reverence for the Tao and its manifestations is essential. The only choice lies in this – either that the meditation be combined with practice of devotion so that they merge, a method favoured by Tibetan teachers especially; or the meditation should be performed at one time of day, devotions at another, both of them *regularly* and without fail.

Nor can meditation be successfully performed in isolation from other kinds of spiritual practice. The adept must purify himself of all gross hindrances and entanglements, disciplining himself in such a manner that the 'I'-delusion withers. Purification entails abstention from over-sleeping, over-eating, the use of intoxicants and so forth, accompanied by a gradual weaning of the mind away from sensual objects. Then, too, there must be cultivation of a lively sense of compassion that makes no distinction between self and other. It is not a matter of conventional morality, for the enemy to be guarded against is not sin, not the flouting of a set of commandments, but whatever tends to inflate the ego. From this point of view, a self-indulgent man may often be seen as a very jolly fellow and liked for being naturally warm-hearted, not as an evil creature; nevertheless, since self-mastery is the very essence of successful meditation, for him to spend much time on it without renouncing his self-indulgences would at best be mildly helpful, at worst completely vain. True, there comes a point when all opposites are found to be illusory, but, for as long as the meditator remains at the level of relative truth, good and bad, wise and foolish are entirely real. A (probably apocryphal) Chinese story is often cited to illustrate this point. A certain abbot, criticised by the half-scandalised, half-envious monks in his charge for alleged licentious conduct, remarked placidly: 'My dear disciples, I give all of you permission to transgress the rules of this community. You are free to do whatever you like if, as I hope, you have succeeded in transcending the realm of opposites. Bring me a pound of needles!' When the needles were brought, he swallowed them with evident relish and withdrew. Finding no harm came to him, his disciples bitterly repented having presumed to admonish a true sage.

For meditation it is necessary to have a quiet place free from the likelihood of disturbance. As to posture, although it is taught that meditation can be performed walking, standing, sitting or lying, the lotus posture is generally favoured. If sitting cross-legged with the feet resting sole-upward upon the thighs is too difficult, then some nearly similar position is acceptable at the start. There should be a comfortable cushion and, preferably, a smaller one placed on top of it in such a way that the buttocks are slightly raised so as to reduce pressure on the legs. The back should be held straight, but never rigidly, with the head almost imperceptibly bowed. The hands should rest in the lap facing upward, one upon the other with the tips of the thumbs touching. The eyes should be nearly but not quite closed, the lips slightly parted, the tongue resting against the base of the upper teeth. After a few moments to make oneself comfortable, perfect stillness must be maintained, the breathing being slow, regular and, above all, silent. With practice this position can be maintained for hours. Indeed, the first of my Tibetan teachers, having fallen into meditation before breakfasting off some fresh wheaten rolls he had been offered, emerged from *samadhi* to discover that the rolls were mouldy. Oblivious of time's passing, he had maintained his meditation for several days! However, for beginners, short periods of not more than half an hour are generally thought best.

Differences of posture among the various sects are usually confined to such small matters as which hand rests on which, the extent to which the eyelids should be parted and the degree of importance attached to the lotus posture as opposed to sitting in 'half-lotus' with one leg resting upon the other, or just cross-legged in tailor fashion. My teachers, both Taoist and Buddhist, were not very particular about posture; some teachers (especially in Japan), however, insist on the full lotus posture, even if the novice has to endure weeks or months of pain. This is because, in the long run, it is the posture that can be comfortably maintained longer than any other; moreover it assists the circulation of the *ch'i* (*prana*, cosmic vitality).

Though the various prerequisites to successful meditation may seem daunting, it should be recalled that the mystic's aim transcends all other aims imaginable! The Buddhist meditator longs to be qualified to rescue the countless beings who, revolving endlessly between birth and death, are tossed helplessly by the waves of life's bitter ocean. Great courage is needed for one who, recognising himself as a puny, transient, ever-changing entity, nevertheless dares to take the great leap into the Void – the calm, still, shining, immaculate, indifferentiated realm of Absolute Reality! In theistic terms, the creature takes upon himself the attainment of conscious union with the Godhead; he seeks to pass beyond the familiar state of relativity and plunge into the being of God – in short to *become* God! Nothing less!

Pure Land Meditation

To many Westerners, for reasons already touched upon, this form of meditation is one that may not have much appeal; but, in China, even the most ardent adherents of Ch'an practice recognise that Pure Land meditation, albeit suited to a different kind of temperament, is no less effective than their own.

There are some Pure Land followers, especially in Japan, who hold the compassion of Amitabha Buddha to be so efficacious that nothing else matters. According to one extreme view, purity of conduct and the exercise of compassion towards fellow beings are unnecessary, since nothing a person born into this decadent age can do will make much difference to his essential unfitness and Amitabha's vow in any case extends as much to the unfit as to the fit – an antinomian view not without its parallels in the history of Christianity. However, the traditional Pure Land doctrine, as taught in China, is that purity and compassion must certainly accompany the main practice of reciting the invocation to Amitabha many thousands of times a day with full concentration. Moreover, it is taught that the recitation will be more effective if, in addition, a particular form of meditation is regularly performed.

Pure Land meditation requires visualisation of the Pure Land as described in the sutras and of the glorious Amitayus form of Amitabha together with his attendant Bodhisattvas, especially Kuanyin. The visualisations set forth in one of the important sutras are incredibly detailed; if its instructions are to be understood literally, they involve, to take just a few examples, visualising a halo the size of billions of universes wherein are ten thousand million *nayutas* (even one *nayuta* is an inconceivable amount) of Buddha-forms and 84,000 marks on the person of Amitayus, *each one of them* with 84,000 excellent characteristics and each of those characteristics sending forth 84,000 rays of light! By visualisation is meant creating a scene so vividly before the mind's eye that one beholds every part of it down to the last colourful detail. In practice, however, much simpler visualisations are substituted. One that becomes easy with practice is to visualise Kuanyin as a lovely being clothed in white garments and standing upon a giant lotus with pink petals open wide. One might suppose this to be sheer self-delusion, were it not that so many devotees do obviously achieve *samadhi* in this manner. The form visualised is after all but a symbol of the ardently desired purity and tranquillity of the Void – Ultimate Reality. As C. G. Jung has made clear, a symbol is far from being a merely arbitrary *sign*, for it has a universal nature of deep and abiding significance. Moreover, since the individual mind and the Buddha-Mind, that is to say pure, undifferentiated Mind, are one, 'self-power' and 'other-power' are of course the same and the experience of their sameness can be more easily achieved by pictorial than by conceptual means, as utilising the former is not hindered by a hankering for things to make logical sense. Meditation transcends conceptual thought. The simple people who at first regard the Pure Land as a place apart and the more sophisticated ones who, like Daisetz Suzuki, recognise that 'the Pure Land is experienced while here' and is in fact unimpeded Mind, comprise two classes of meditator who are equally capable of successful achievement. Indeed, unsophisticated adepts often succeed more rapidly, their minds being less cluttered with intellectual litter.

I remember discussing this form of meditation with an old Chinese lady who, with a couple of elderly companions, had retired to a small mountain hermitage to pass her remaining years in holy tranquillity. Built on Lantao Island, Hong Kong, it lay near a pilgrim path that has since become the bus road to Pao Lin Monastery which, in those days, was still a pleasant, simple place. Gratefully drinking her Six Happiness tea, I gazed at a trio of gilded wooden statues that stood on a shelf facing her doorway, representing Amitabha and his attendant Bodhisattvas. Struck by their beauty, I ventured a question which led to her serenely announcing her certainty of being reborn in a lotus bud floating in a jewelled lake which would presently unfold its petals to reveal the Pure Land lying all about her. Then Amitabha or her beloved Kuanyin would compassionately instruct her in the truths of impermanence and egolessness until all evil karma resulting from her past lives had been swallowed up in wisdom, leaving her unfettered mind free to enter Nirvana's peace. From the way she expressed herself I knew that she fully expected to behold marvellous trees bedecked with jewelled fruit and leaves, lakes and pavilions lovely to the eye and emitting rays more brilliant than a myriad suns and moons. The old lady had long ago managed to commit to memory the whole of the sutra in which these wonders are described and could recite it by heart. It was very touching; but, being then still sceptical about the Pure Land method, I voiced my doubts obliquely, saying something like: 'How happy you must be to have this assurance of being reborn in the Pure Land. Surely you must be envied by Buddhists of other sects who undergo all sorts of austerities just in the hope of securing a propitious rebirth still within life's bitter ocean?'

Smiling pleasantly, she answered: 'Well, I suppose there are lots of people so rich in learning and merit that an old creature like me would cut a poor figure beside them, but I do my best. You must not think winning rebirth in the Pure Land is an easy matter. It is Buddha's compassion, not our own merits, that draws us there. But how would his compassion reach us if we were lost in selfishness? It would find nothing to hook onto. I hope to obtain it because for years I have not tasted the flesh of poor creatures done to death for my pleasure or milk stolen from the calves who should be feeding on it happily. If we did not get rid of harsh thoughts, cruel words, envy and the like, our minds would be so clouded that we should not recognise purity if we saw it. It is only by kindness and generosity that we manage to do down that old *mara* (devil) – self!'

All this was said very simply and with obvious sincerity. I left that wayside hermitage with much food for thought, having been especially struck by her figure of speech, 'nothing to hook onto'. Clearly her version of the Pure Land doctrine was no mechanical method of liberation. She might believe literally in the reality of those jewelled lakes and trees, but the need for the self-discipline and compassion she exercised in the hope of beholding them seemed to her no less real. I recognised that they would assuredly purify her mind and have the same ego-negating effect as if she were someone with a much more subtle conception of the Pure Land.

Years after that chance meeting, I met a monk in Peking who explained the matter thus: 'The sutra (Wu-Liang Shou Ching) describing the beauties of the Pure Land speaks in metaphors. Each of its picturesque details has a precise esoteric meaning; they are not made up like the background of a fairy story for children, but correspond to what is or will be found in the meditator's mind. My own teacher was fond of explaining them one by one, but he taught that there was no real need to know those things; as the meditation progresses over months and years, they become clear of themselves. If, at the beginning, one tried to explain too much, people would be awed by the difficulty and be afraid to meditate. How sad that would be and how culpable the teacher responsible! With our Pure Land meditation, the simplicity of the meditator is of no importance; so long as the devotee meditates whole-heartedly, the result will be the same no matter how simple his original conceptions.'

The Pure Land doctrine is also widely current in Tibet among those who find tantric paths too steep; but, since the sutras make mention of vast numbers of Pure Lands, realms other than Amitabha's are often chosen as being easier to enter, or else harder but more swiftly rewarding in terms of full illumination. Recently someone told me that she had overheard a Tibetan say jokingly: 'Oh, I wouldn't choose Amitabha Buddha's Pure Land. It must be overflowing with Chinese!' The realm dearest to the Tibetan heart is Tara's Potala, which rises amidst the sea, a sure refuge from life's ocean of sorrow. In Tibet, Avalokitesvara Bodhisattva (identified by the Chinese with Kuanyin) is always depicted in male form, Tara being a female emanation 'born of a tear shed by Avalokitesvara'; so those who feel instinctively that a female form best typifies the quality of divine compassion naturally become devotees of Tara in one of her twenty-one forms. Where specifically tantric meditation is concerned, visualisation of any being as an object of reverence *separate* from the meditator is held to be suited only to contemplatives still at an elementary stage of understanding. At the higher levels, the figure visualised is not static; it ultimately merges with the meditator and they are felt as one – mind absorbed in Mind!

Ch'an (Zen) and Mahamudra Meditation

Ch'an started with a smile. Once Shakyamuni Buddha held up a flower in silence, a gesture that was understood by only one of his disciples, Mahakasyapa, who responded by smiling his recognition of 'the reality that is not seen' but silently communicated from mind to mind. Later, he in turn transmitted this mind-to-mind perception to a long line of patriarchs until, in the sixth century A.D., it was brought to China. There, as a 'teaching without words' it commended itself to those who were steeped in Taoist doctrine and was transmitted down a line of six Chinese patriarchs, whereafter the patriarchal transmission ceased and several separate streams of Ch'an came into being, some of which found their way to Japan where a number of sub-sects of Zen now flourish. Though doctrinally Ch'an has never departed from orthodox Mahayana philosophy, its characteristic methods and cryptic modes of expression owe much to Taoism, whose adherents display a similar love of paradox. Like the higher reaches of the Vajrayana in Tibet, Ch'an is essentially a Short Path doctrine. Though it is normally held well nigh impossible to achieve Enlightenment within one lifetime, Ch'an and the Vajrayana set out to do just that! Therefore Ch'an, though by no means as opposed to rites and other devotional practices as has sometimes been suggested, concentrates above all on meditation – hence its Chinese and Japanese names, both of which signify '*dhyana*' (meditation). By the use of paradox and eccentricities, it aims at shocking the adept into experiencing a sudden revelation of the ultimate nature of being as pure Mind – sudden in the sense that, although years may have to be spent in preparing for this intuitive experience, it finally bursts upon him like a flash of light.

In Japan, the Rinzai branch of Zen makes great use of a technique known as the *koan* (Chinese, *kung-an* or *hua-t'ou*), a *koan* being a conundrum which defies logical solution and drives the mind beyond conceptual thought. It may consist of one sentence such as 'What is the sound of one hand clapping?' or take the form of a little story, thus: 'Someone asked: "When the entire body disintegrates, something everlastingly spiritual remains – what is it?" to which the Master replied: "It's windy again this morning." ' Obviously there is no *logical* answer to the question about clapping, nor a *logical* connection between the second question and the answer given. Though such *koans* largely originated in China, it is mostly in Japan that hundreds of them are systematically employed to suit people, time and circumstance; in Chinese monasteries, the use of a great variety of *koans* and the emphasis put upon that method are held to be productive of yet further obstacles to illumination; only two have been widely used, either 'Who reverences the Buddha?' meaning 'Who really am I?', or 'What was my original face before my father and mother were born?' which has essentially the same meaning. Such conundrums can either be shot at the pupil, who must answer before he has time to think, or be pondered day and night during long hours of meditation. Sometimes blows, shouts or bursts of incomprehensible laughter are used by the teacher to bring the meaning home and give rise to sudden illumination.

The recent widespread Western interest in Ch'an (Zen) owes much to the appeal of such unconventional 'shock tactics' and also to the sect's seeming iconoclasm, as when Master Hui Hai (without the least intention of belittling the Buddha) exclaimed, 'The sage seeks from mind, not from the Buddha; the fool seeks from the Buddha, not from mind!' or as exemplified by the anecdote applauding a monk who chopped up a wooden image of the Buddha to provide a fire against the cold of a winter's night. However, *koans* and startling behaviour are not necessarily an integral part of Ch'an; some branches of the sect make no use of them at all. The essence of the doctrine is that mind is the key to Enlightenment; so long as a person's mind is a prey to delusion, he will forever be forging new chains of karma. The One Mind, also known as the Buddha-Mind, is a Ch'an (Zen) synonym for the Tao; in meditation it is necessary to grasp this Mind and perceive its identity with that which meditates. Mind is the root. Contemplating our original nature (Mind) is the core of the practice. As Master Hui Hai once put it:

Q: Whereon should the mind settle and dwell?
A: It should settle upon non-dwelling and there dwell.
Q: What is this non-dwelling?
A: It means not allowing the mind to dwell on anything whatso-ever.
Q: And what is the meaning of that?
A: Dwelling upon nothing means that the mind is not fixed upon good or evil, being or non-being, inside or outside or somewhere between the two, void or non-void, concentration or distraction. This dwelling upon nothing is the state in which it should dwell; those who attain to it are said to have non-dwelling minds – in other words, they have Buddha-Mind!
Q: What does mind resemble?
A: Mind has no colour, such as green or yellow, red or white; it is not long or short; it does not vanish or appear; it is free from purity and impurity alike; and its duration is eternal. It is utter stillness. Such, then, is the form and shape of our original mind, which is also our original body – the Buddha-Body!

Ch'an meditation involves total relinquishment of all dualistic concepts, so that all pairs of opposites are perceived to be void; nor must the thought arise: 'Now *I* see that all opposites are void and have relinquished them', since 'I' and 'relinquished' are themselves opposites of 'other' and 're-tained'. The mind must be used like a great mirror that reflects the passing show without the least attachment. Not blind to good and evil, one must remain without love or aversion for either. One's mind must be unaffected by the arising and vanishing of environmental forms, so that it remains void and motionless, just dealing with the moment's needs and then letting them go – this is what is termed 'being never apart from the Buddha'; it is also very close to the Taoists' *wu-wei*. Achieving this result may be helped by the use of a *koan*, but the *koan* must never be allowed to obstruct direct perception, as may happen.

In most of the Chinese monasteries I visited, there was a shrine-hall where the monks assembled twice daily for devotional rites and also a meditation-hall where the contemplative section of the community resided. The latter was generally a square chamber with an octagonal shrine (dedicated to Manjusri Bodhisattva, embodiment of the Buddha-Wisdom) in the centre and a very wide platform running along all four walls but leaving plenty of floor-space around the shrine. At night, the contemplative monks would sleep side by side on the platform; by day, the bedding would be rolled up and replaced by square cushions on which, during meditation periods, they would sit in the lotus position facing away from the wall. A typical session would begin with ten minutes of quiet sitting, a time for banishing wayward thoughts and letting the mind grow still. Then *bok*! At this stroke of the wooden-fish drum, all would rise and perambulate the shrine to the rhythm of its *bok-bok-bok* of which the tempo gradually increased until they were hurrying round, shoulders hunched in the ritual manner, never quite breaking into a run. BOK! Everyone would stop dead. *Bok-bok* was the signal to make for the nearest meditation cushion. Taking up the lotus posture as before, the monks would wait for a single chime from the preceptor's silver bell, whereupon the intensive part of the meditation would begin, unless the preceptor had a few words of instruction for the younger monks present. Thereafter there would be unbroken silence and the meditation would proceed for as long as it took for a slow-burning stick of incense to burn out. Meanwhile two monks would pad round the room carrying wooden broadswords euphemistically known as 'perfumed boards' with which to smite the shoulders of those who fell asleep or became lost in a daze, either painlessly with the flat of the blade or, in the case of persistent backsliding, soundlessly and painfully with the edge. When the incense had burned away, the perambulation would be repeated, followed by another round of meditation. Other rounds might follow and, at certain times of the year, occupy some twenty hours each day, meals being served to the monks where they sat, with no one permitted to leave the hall except during the brief intervals allowed for urination. This, then, was the form of communal Ch'an-style meditation. What of its content?

The content is much more difficult to describe. If the *hua-t'ou* 'Nien Fu shih sei?' ('Who reverences the Buddha?') was used, mere repetition would of course have been meaningless, but so would an attempt to solve the problem logically. Or rather, a beginner would probably employ logical deduction in the early stages, dismissing the possible concomitants of the seeming 'I' in turn – not the body, nor any part of it, not memory, nor feeling, nor personality and so on. 'Not that, not that, not that, then what? Consciousness? But who is the owner of that consciousness? *Who* in fact is the one who is conscious? A dead end!' No matter how stale the subject, how tired the mind and body, the relentless enquiry would be pursued. At last, all logical possibilities having been eliminated, a change would occur; the mind would cease to wrestle logically with the conundrum and intuition would be aroused. Up to this point, it was as though one had been hurling questions at some other being within himself, propounding them over and over again – a thousand times, ten thousand times – as though to drive the fellow to distraction, exasperating him into revealing his identity. With the arising of some glimmer of intuition, fatigues, frustration, boredom would give way to something pleasurable, exciting even, then blissful. The mind having finally abandoned concepts would have somehow slipped into another mode, a different level of consciousness. And from there?

Beyond that lies the realm of the indescribable. Dimness recedes before the dawning of direct perception of the Void.

Concepts such as 'I' and 'other' have lost their meaning. A vast, unborn, unending unity is sensed, perhaps shadowy or intermittent at first, then clearer, brighter or immediately glorious – a pure emptiness lovelier than all the radiant forms and colours in the world!

I believe that what the Japanese Zen Masters call *satori* (the Chinese use the equivalent term, *chieh-wu*, more sparingly) must apply to anything from a small, sudden shift in the mode of consciousness up to, at the end of a whole progression of *satoris*, what is termed Supreme Unexcelled Enlightenment. If so, experience of the earlier *satoris*, though striking enough in itself, should by no means be confused with that ultimate experience. The Chinese Masters, on the whole, seem less convinced that a whole series of *sudden* leaps occurs. However, it is true that, at a relatively early stage, the adept may be visited by at least a limited intuition of the voidness of all seeming entities, including the so-called 'self'. Henceforth, when he speaks of voidness, egolessness and so forth, he is speaking of something experienced at a deeper level of consciousness than that of logic and conceptual thought, though perhaps still a billion, billion *yojanas* removed from the Supreme Unexcelled Enlightenment of a Buddha! Just at what point understanding parts company from what has previously been conceived intellectually and becomes pure intuitive experience is hard to say; one may, I think, imagine he has attained a minor degree of *satori* long before pure intuition takes over, especially if he has read accounts of what is expected to happen. Therefore one should hesitate before affirming that he has experienced *satori* and before accepting such an affirmation from others. To say nothing of truly Enlightened Beings – Buddhas! – even an adept who has experienced only a very limited degree of illumination is aware of the futility and impropriety of talking about it. And, if ever a person is heard to claim that he has 'achieved Enlightenment'(!), his making such a statement is a certain indication that he has not!

In recent years, hundreds of thousands of words have been

written about the so-called 'wordless doctrine' and its practice. Well and good; if nothing had been written about it, most of the world would never have heard of its existence; even so, I believe there is much more to be gained from reading and re-reading translations of texts by actual Ch'an (Zen) Masters, and of course the marvellous Diamond Sutra and Heart Sutra, than from studying books written around and about this difficult subject. Since an Enlightened Master can find no way of conveying even a tithe of his *own* direct experience in words, how much the less can others say much that is of value! The following anecdote about Bodhidharma is well worth pondering: 'Said Bodhidharma to Hui K'ê (his successor to the Ch'an patriarchy): "Bring me your mind and let me quiet it." To this Hui K'ê replied: "I cannot find it." Whereat Bodhidharma proclaimed: "I have now quieted your mind!" ' (A mind resting tranquilly in the No-Where of the Void would naturally be free from self-awareness and therefore nowhere to be found; how otherwise could it be said to be in the Void?)

Within the great range of practices which Tibetan lamas teach for use at different stages is one called Mahamudra that is a close counterpart of Ch'an. True, no *koan* is used; but then, in China and Japan, only some teachers set much store by the *koan* technique. The Tibetan pupil, having been taught how to banish wayward thoughts by the attainment of one-pointedness, is then set the task of seeking his original mind by the same progression from rational to intuitive processes that one finds in Ch'an, so that he comes to perceive the Void and, though aware of what transpires around him, remains thenceforth unattached. Whole passages of *The Tibetan Yoga of Knowing the Mind*, one of the profound works edited by Evans Wentz, read exactly like the writings of Ch'an Masters except for their more solemn style – a solemnity often counterbalanced by the oral teaching of the lamas, which is likely to be full of paradox and humour. The work just referred to – there are many of its kind – begins with a salutation to the One Mind that embraces the whole of samsara and Nirvana, and proceeds to equate this One Mind with the Buddha-Essence, the 'All-Foundation', which is a synonym for Sunyata, the Void. It is full of typically Ch'an-style pronouncements, such as 'Realisation of the One Mind constitutes the All-Deliverence'. This might be taken as evidence of direct Chinese influence on the Tibetan author of this book of yoga; however, within the fold of mysticism, such 'co-incidences' abound, being attributable not necessarily to cross-influences, but to similar experiences encountered by mystics in their search for intuitive realisation.

Another and different Tibetan method is described in the section on Tantric Meditation with which this chapter ends.

T'ien T'ai Meditation

T'ien T'ai adepts, for all that they attach great importance to learning so as to build up a deep intellectual understanding of the profound principles of the Dharma, are very keen exponents of meditation and their system is often regarded as the most advanced of all the Chinese systems, or at least the most thorough. Never have they advocated learning for its own sake, but always as a valuable support for meditation. Not having met a T'ien T'ai teacher, I have unfortunately had no opportunity of studying that system at first hand; but I have both heard and read something of the famous *chih-kuan* method.

By *chih* is meant 'halting', putting an end to the aimless wandering of the mind and thus transcending conceptual thought. *Kuan* denotes awareness, reflection, observation, self-examination. It is taught that those who cultivate *chih* alone get lost in the bliss of *samadhi* and make no further progress; and that cultivation of *kuan* alone leads to wisdom but no further; so they must be practised turn by turn. *Chih* is performed by such methods as counting the breaths, or attending to the play of inhalation and exhalation upon the tips of the nostrils, or concentrating on a fixed point such as the tip of the nose. *Kuan* involves turning the mind inward upon itself, reflecting on the emptiness of the 'self' and other entities, contemplating the purity of the undifferentiated Void and thus achieving intuitive experience of matters already understood up to a point intellectually. Detailed instruction is given as to means of perceiving the void nature of the different aspects of the realm of form. When and how often one should turn from *chih* to *kuan* and *vice versa* depends upon the needs of the meditator, his tendencies, state of mind and so forth. The beginner, finding that *chih* gives rise to bliss, may be inclined to linger in that state; if his mind is naturally torpid, he will find that *chih* is easier than *kuan*; therefore he must pay increased attention to the latter. The intellectual may be afraid or scornful of *chih*, wrongly supposing it will prove to be a kind of fruitless trance-state, a dulling of the mind's keen blade; whereas he may delight in the analytical examination of the phenomena engaging his mind; such a man needs to learn that intuitive wisdom arises only when the mind is still. With practice, he will discover how to alternate the two states in a manner productive of real progress.

The instructions for T'ien T'ai meditation are often so detailed and subtle as to be daunting. Also there are formidable prerequisites – complete severance from all worldly occupations, retirement to a cave or remote hermitage, very strict control of diet and sleep. The mind and body must be purified, the adept being very sensible of shame at his short-comings and firmly determined to eliminate them.

I do not know if there is a close Tibetan equivalent of the T'ien T'ai Sect, but its austerity is reminiscent of the conduct of Tibetan Kargyupas, of whom the poet Milarepa is probably the best known in the West. Kargyupas are noted for spending long years in well-nigh uninterrupted meditation, preferably in mountain caves, and for very austere living. It is not uncommon for them to live in strict seclusion for three years, seven years or indeed a lifetime, avoiding speech with those who bring them food and living on such spartan foods as nettles. Yet, as can be gauged from the biography of Milarepa and from his poems, they are joyful men, not sanctimonious or prudish but with a sometimes prankish sense of humour. Since the lives of T'ien T'ai and Kargyupa adepts are so austere and mere frivolity so foreign to their nature, whence do they derive their joy, if not from what is perceived and experienced during meditation? I have sometimes been repelled by accounts of the lives of men esteemed holy in other parts of the world; so often they seem to have been stern or even gloomy men, tight-lipped and prone to frown and thunder. I have never found this true of Chinese or Tibetan holy men, no matter how many years they have passed in seclusion or undergoing austerities; those who have progressed far along the path are easily recognisable by an air of gentle gaiety and smiling tolerance that makes one certain they have discovered a fount of joy within themselves.

Tantric Meditation

The theory and practice of tantric methods properly belong to the next chapter, but it would not do for this account of the path of meditation to exclude entirely one of the most powerful and effective meditational techniques of all.

Since the Chinese Esoteric Sect (Mi Tsung) became extinct centuries ago for a reason to be explained later, its place in Chinese Buddhism has been taken by the Vajrayana (tantric) School whose teachings were long disseminated in many parts of China by Tibetan and Mongol lamas. Initiates into the methods of this Short Path system are enjoined to be discreet in transmitting them to others; however, the one now briefly to be described has already appeared in several English works – often, alas, in distorted form. If my account of it seems bald or the method itself too akin in appearance to magic to deserve serious consideration, that is because the conceptions on which it is based are so foreign to our accustomed way of thinking that an acceptable description would require whole chapters of introductory material; perhaps what is said in the next chapter will put the matter in a somewhat clearer light.

The essence of this tantric method is to start with visualisation of an appropriate being; the body, speech and mind of the adept must then be united with the Body, Speech and Mind of that which is visualised; then both adept and object are merged and finally 'banished' so that nothing is left but pure Mind resting in stillness. The being visualised may be a Bodhisattva, an embodiment of some Buddha-Quality of a kind common to all Mahayana sects, or else an embodiment of one of the adept's own energies with which he sets out to destroy delusions, passions and inordinate desires. The chosen object may be visualised in lovely, tranquil form or in a form appallingly ferocious when the purpose is to combat anger, lust and so forth by means of the very energies that they arouse.

One begins with devotional rites, saluting first his teacher, then the Buddha, Dharma (Doctrine) and Sangha (Sacred Community) and making offerings of incense, flowers, lights, pure water and other symbolic objects. Next come certain preliminary reflections aimed at arousing remorse for past un-skilful conduct, lively compassion for the innumerable beings still lost in delusion, gratitude to the teachers of the Dharma and a great thirst for speedy liberation. All of these are held to induce a suitable state of mind for the main practice. Now the object of meditation, whether the aspect evoked is tranquil or wrathful, is visualised in the clearest detail possible – colour, garments, ornaments, posture, gesture and so on all having deep symbolic significance. At first the visualised being is held to be a mere likeness similar to a picture or a statue; but, as the contemplative rite proceeds, the meditator's own energies of body, speech and mind are caused to merge with what, at the level of relative truth, is conceived of as 'other-power'; the visualised form now becomes endowed with mental, oral and physical characteristics. If the visualisation is centred upon Avalokitesvara (the male counterpart of the Chinese Kuanyin), the visualised form now *becomes* that Bodhisattva, who as yet remains separate from the meditator. This completes the first stage, during which, if the adept is skilled, he beholds Avalokitesvara as clearly as the furnishings upon his altar, the walls and ceiling of the room.

The second stage begins with visualising in the heart of Avalokitesvara a *dharani* or sequence of shining syllables revolving round a central 'seed-syllable' representing the essence of that Bodhisattva's being. As the syllables revolve, the adept perceives them clearly and intones their sound, perhaps 108 or 1,080 or even 10,800 times.

At the third stage, the Bodhisattva, form no bigger than the top section of a man's thumb, is visualised as entering through the crown of the adept's head and coming to rest in his heart, whereupon the latter feels himself growing smaller and smaller until he and the Bodhisattva are exactly coterminous, perfectly united, in no sense separate. Having merged with Avalokitesvara, embodiment of the Buddha-Compassion, he now feels empowered to direct towards sentient beings streams of compassion imbued with actual beneficial power. Next the adept (who is also the Bodhisattva) feels himself dissolving, his outer parts contracting into the centre of his being until nothing is left but the heart. The heart dissolves into the circle of moving syllables within, the syllables into the seed-syllable they surround, the main body of this syllable into its apex, the apex into a point, the point into infinite Void and deep *samadhi* is attained.

To those accustomed to less elaborate kinds of meditation, this powerful method may seem over-complicated and doubt may be felt as to whether the figure visualised in fact becomes endowed (and thus able to endow the adept) with the Body, Speech and Mind of the Bodhisattva. Indeed the method is elaborate and the merging of 'self-power' with 'other-power' is of course not susceptible of proof, but there is no doubt whatever that, as a means of attaining *samadhi*, the practice – *works*! It is assuredly not suited to all types of meditator and may be particularly unsuited to those who have yet to overcome the hindrances posed by a well developed logical faculty or by being unable to recognise that imagination and so-called reality, both being born of mind, are not different in quality; on the other hand, some of those who have spent years cultivating less esoteric methods with only meagre results find this tantric mode of meditation most marvellously effective. Everything depends upon the outlook, personality and understanding of the meditator. My fear lest the accounts given in this chapter of various forms of meditation do them but scant justice is especially strong in the case of the tantric method. How I wish I could convey the full splendour and effectiveness of every one of them!

Chapter 7

The Esoteric Path
Tantric Buddhism

Going for the first time from 'the Eighteen Provinces' (China Proper) into one of the Tibetan and Mongol border regions was like visiting another world. Whereas elsewhere in China pious Buddhists formed a relatively small minority, in those border regions it would have been difficult to find among the local people any whose lives were not permeated by faith in Buddhism; but how strange was the imagery in their temples! Besides statues and paintings of benign Buddhas and Bodhisattvas portrayed in the usual manner as tranquil beings of exalted, other-worldly beauty, what a wealth of fantastically bizarre figures – Buddhas and their Dakinis locked in sexual embrace, fierce and wrathful Buddhas, to say nothing of male and female divinities of extraordinary aspect, some with just one eye in the middle of the forehead, some with a thousand eyes gazing from every part of their anatomy; some with heads like those of bulls but brilliantly coloured, innumerable hands clutching hideous weapons or grasping such grisly trophies as a skull-cup brimming with blood and brains, bodies adorned with necklaces of skulls or freshly severed human heads, feet dancing upon mounds of corpses! How easy it would have been to be revolted by this vivid and terrifying symbolism! For a time I was deeply disquieted and would have been astounded had anyone foretold that I was destined to embrace this form of Buddhism and would one day recognise those baleful-seeming beings as the august and compassionate friends of those who follow the Way!

My first encounter with the world of lamas, prayer-flags and gigantic prayer-wheels took place when I was twenty-two years old during a long summer visit to Mount Wu T'ai, which stands close to the boundary between North China and Inner Mongolia. I ought to have been better prepared for what I saw there, having been initiated to some extent into the inner purpose of tantric Buddhism by a Tibetan lama who, very soon after my arrival in the East, had remained for some weeks in Hong Kong instructing some of my Chinese friends in the Vajrayana (tantric) tradition; but, owing to language difficulties, I had taken in only a little of what he taught – a misfortune that did not disconcert the lama, for he smilingly remarked: 'The seeds I have sown in your mind will bear fruit when the time for their ripening has come.'

In those days, Mount Wu T'ai was a truly marvellous place, exotic beyond a traveller's wildest dreams. Never, before or since, have I seen anywhere to compare with it for sheer colourfulness, and the months I spent there were undoubtedly among the happiest in my life. Though the civil authorities were Chinese, the population consisted largely of several thousand Mongols (mostly monks) under the spiritual direction of a high monastic dignitary sent from Lhasa. Half way up the mountain is a broad grassy plateau from which rise five separate peaks (some 8,000 feet high) from which it takes its name – Mountain of Five Terraces. At the time of my visit, there were about three hundred temples, large and small, and reflections of the medieval splendour of Tibet still lingered. In summer the whole scene was ablaze with colour, for the temples with their terracotta or yellow walls, white *chortens* (reliquary towers) and richly lacquered arches and gateways stood for the most part upon the plateau, where bloomed acre upon acre of wild flowers sparkling like multicoloured gems; nor was this all, for on festival days there were processions of dignitaries clad in maroon and yellow monastic garb or in gorgeously embroidered robes like those worn by courtiers in the Forbidden City at the height of Peking's imperial glory.

Colour, colour everywhere! With a young Chinese companion I lodged at P'usa Ting, the principal monastery; the great chamber allotted to us had to be seen to be believed. About half the space was occupied by a wide platform covered with rich Tibetan carpets and enclosed on three sides by walls embellished with brightly coloured murals; the other half, floored with red tiles, was furnished with gaily lacquered cabinets, chairs and tables. Living there as we did for several months made me feel like a fairy-story prince – a feeling in which I was young enough to revel. I suppose such unmonastic luxury had originally been intended for great Chinese and Manchu dignitaries from Peking; but, by then, the Celestial Empire had long been swept away and distinguished visitors had become so rare that these splendours were granted to ordinary travellers like myself.

Wandering from temple to temple, as yet too weak in Chinese to profit from what might have been taught me, I was continually struck by the terrifying iconography. Perhaps because Mount Wu T'ai with its five peaks resembles the arrangement lying at the heart of tantric mandalas

it is sacred to Manjusri Bodhisattva (Wen Shû, in Chinese), embodiment of the Buddha-Wisdom, whose statue occupied a prominent place in most of the temples there. Usually he was depicted riding on a lion, carrying a book (representing the Buddha Dharma) in one hand and, in the other, an upraised sword with which to slice through the bonds of ignorance and delusion. His face was sometimes that of a lovely youth, but more often of a mature, lightly bearded scholar, and in both these forms he looked inspiring; yet, somewhere near at hand there would always be a picture of him in the ferocious form of Yamantaka, Conqueror of Death – a blue-skinned, multiheaded monster with countless limbs, his principal head that of a fanged and horned bull, the other heads equally bizarre, except for the tiny, serenely smiling Buddha-head that crowned them all. Clasped to his breast were a knife and skull-cup filled with blood, and his many other hands grasped an assortment of dreadful weapons. Dangling from his neck were ropes of human heads and his feet trampled corpses both human and animal, his whole person being encircled by lurid flames. But for the one small Buddha-head and the sacred lotus throne beneath his feet, there was nothing to recall the gentle, violence-abhoring Buddha of whose tranquil wisdom Manjusri (and therefore Yamantaka) was held to be an embodiment. To see Manjusri in this form was to understand why travellers have described what they found in Tibet and Mongolia as 'a monstrous travesty of Buddhism'. I was inclined, at the time, to think the same. As yet, I had very little understanding of such matters.

Such representations of wrathful deities and the no less astonishing depictions of Buddhas and Dakinis locked in ecstatic embrace had been largely responsible for the demise, some centuries before, of the Mi Tsung, a native Chinese esoteric sect devoted to tantric practice. It was easy to see why the Chinese, whose conventional Confucian training had made them fastidious and opposed to everything excessive, had rejected it. Indeed the Confucian authorities must have been scandalised by an iconography that depicted sexual union in a religious context. Quite recently I came to learn that the Japanese Shingon Sect (an offshoot of the defunct Mi Tsung) seems at one time to have had a similar iconography, though there are few traces of it now. Well, *religious* sexual symbolism excites as much repugnance in the average Chinese or Japanese as in the breast of a pious Scots Presbyterian, so it is not to be wondered at that tantric Buddhism had failed, on the whole, to take firm root in China Proper and Japan (although many Chinese individuals practised it).

Although the Mongol lamas and laymen I met on Mount Wu T'ai were extremely kind and anxious to make me feel welcome, it was sometimes a relief to visit Kuang-chi Mou-p'ang, a Chinese monastery in the vicinity where the Abbot, Master

Nêng Hai, having studied in Lhasa for several years, was expounding tantric teachings to Chinese monks whose ignorance of the Mongol and Tibetan languages made it difficult to study under the local lamas. I felt very much more at home in that familiar milieu of grey-robed monks, typically Chinese architecture and a monastic way of life similar to that elsewhere in China. Also I made friends with a party of Chinese laymen lodging there. They were visitors like myself who had journeyed for a whole week from the nearest rail-head, following the lonely road leading into the mountains, some on foot, others on horseback or in litters carried by a pair of mules harnessed to shafts before and behind. Devout, yet merry and unsanctimonious, they addressed one another (and me) by the title Bodhisattva, not from the arrogant assumption of being already among the elect – such an attitude is unknown in Buddhist circles – but as a way of showing respect for the Bodhisattva Vow each of us had taken, the vow to aim at Enlightenment for the sake of assisting other sentient beings to liberate themselves from samsara's bonds, rather than as a means of attaining Nirvana's peace.

But this seemingly typical Chinese monastery was not as ordinary as it looked. One evening these friends took me to an upper room where we found Master Nêng Hai and his disciples seated erect upon Tibetan-style floor-cushions, wholly absorbed in ejaculating over and over again with cheerful energy the mantra: 'Yamantaka HUM PHAT!' How strange it seemed, how utterly alien to those Chinese surroundings, to find intelligent and learned men thus engaged, especially as it transpired that they devoted hours each evening to that exotic practice!

Several years were to pass before I came to appreciate the power of mantras to produce heightened states of consciousness (and much else besides!) or to know that those skilled in their use can, in a few minutes or seconds, achieve what otherwise requires long periods of sustained meditation. Meanwhile the meaning of what I had seen that evening, like so much else on the sacred mountain, remained a mystery.

From my long stay on Mount Wu T'ai I carried away a jumble of impressions, not the least of which was respect and affection for the Tibetans and Mongols I had come to know there. Surely, I reflected, there must be a great deal to be said for religious beliefs which, however weird, excite such devotion and have the effect of making people so kindly and good-humoured. In the years that followed, I took every possible opportunity to learn more of this form of Buddhism, first from Tibetan and Mongol lamas living in China, later by visiting such places as Sikkim and Tibetan enclaves in the Himalayan foot-hills lying within India's frontiers. In my quest for under-standing I was greatly helped by what for Tibetans was a supremely tragic situation; the fate which had overwhelmed their country had led to an exodus of learned and saintly men who had become accessible in greater numbers than ever before. My including something of what I learnt from them in a book dealing principally with mysticism in China is fully justified by the fact that Tibetan-style tantric Buddhism had been firmly established in certain Chinese Buddhist circles for centuries, probably ever since the passing away of the native Chinese Esoteric Sect (Mi Tsung). It therefore forms part of the overall picture of Chinese Buddhism as it existed during the years I spent in that country.

The Vajrayana, to give tantric Buddhism its formal name, is first and foremost a 'Short Path' doctrine aiming at Enlighten-ment in this very life, always with the purpose of undertaking the Bodhisattva's task of liberating other sentient beings from aeons of rebirth into samsara's bitter ocean. It is because a liberator must himself be free that Vajrayana adepts set store by powerful means of attaining Enlightenment within a single life-span. Being powerful, the means are also dangerous. Wrongly employed, they destroy those who use them as surely as high voltage current destroys those who operate it without taking suitable precautions. Therefore study of the Vajrayana is hedged about with difficulties. Having first found a teacher and won his confidence, one embarks upon the arduous yogic meditations and exercises that must precede each successive initiation. The need for initiations and the secrecy attending them are not, as is sometimes supposed, dictated by a desire to veil certain rites, texts and symbols that non-initiates would deem improper; not prudery (a state of mind Tibetans would find laughable) but the caution proper to the use of powerful and dangerous means of cultivation is the cause.

In essence those means consist of using the energy engendered by all things, good, bad and indifferent, to destroy hindrances to swift realisation – passion to destroy passion, desire to destroy desire and so on. There must be a shattering transformation of evil propensities that nevertheless leaves the energy they generate intact for use in overcoming obstacles, achieving the union of opposites and thus attaining the direct experiential self-realisation in which the self is voided. Hence the ferocious aspect of those beings depicted as drinking blood and dancing upon corpses, for they are no other than externalisations of the terrible powers needed for self-conquest. In tantric meditation they are visualised with a zeal that makes them live. Every detail has a significance that must be understood not just intellectually but as part of a profound intuitive experience. In making assaults upon the persistent ego-consciousness, one is bound to encounter horrors beyond the power of sculptor or painter to portray. The ego, though ultimately a delusion, has been nourished by life after life spent in pandering to its demands. Capable of the utmost vileness, endowed with fearful energy, it has ten thousand ways of avenging itself upon its would-be destroyer. On more gradual paths to liberation, the ego can be slowly eroded by sustained compassion, self-discipline and self-analysis of mind, but the Short Path adept, seeking to obliterate it by direct assault, must be armed with fiery energy and implacable determination. The severed heads hanging from Yamantaka's neck, the corpses he tramples are the ego-aspects which the adept has systematically uprooted; the surrounding flames, his baneful mien and horrid weapons represent the ferocious energy required to achieve the ego's swift conquest. By visualising his form, this energy is first portrayed, then actualised and turned unrelentingly upon ego-engendered passions and desires. Just how this can be so becomes clear only with actual practice in performing the yoga; it would be very difficult to convey in words.

Tantric yoga also involves recognition of the male and female components of the adept's being; everyone, possessing as he does a body that is a replica of the macrocosm, inevitably contains these contrasting components (as the *yinyang* philosophers were well aware); their harmonisation forms an important part of the path to self-realisation. Moreover, the practice pertains, though at a different level, to the union of Wisdom (the goal) and Compassion (the means), which are symbolised during rituals by the officiant's *vajra*-wand (representing the adamantine nature of the unchanging Void and the means for its realisation) and *vajra*-bell (symbolising supreme intuitive Wisdom); the shapes of these implements have a sexual connotation, symbolising the perfect union between means and goal. This same concept is also expressed by *Yabyum* (Father-Mother) figures in sexual embrace. It was this symbology that the Chinese and Japanese found so shocking when it was introduced among them – but is it truly shocking? In dealing with the tremendous, more-than-life-and-death matter of annihilating the ego and realising perfect union with the Tao, the Ultimate, is there any place for prudery? What more appropriate and vivid a symbol can there be than that of figures lost in the bliss of self-transcending union to represent the merging of opposites, the obliteration of the delusion of self and other, the final culmination of intense longing?

Those who tread this yogic path must undergo formidable training. Preparation for the required transformation of mind generally requires that several years be passed continuously meditating in solitary confinement and one of the specific yoga practices, *tummo*, involves sitting stark naked amidst snow and ice in the cruel Tibetan winter! This is no path for weaklings or libertines; long years of rigid self-discipline must precede the use of energy generated by the fires of anger, greed and lust to quench those passions. Naturally, even in Tibet, there are only comparatively few who pursue this rugged path.

The preparation for Enlightenment has also a warmly appealing side, the whole tantric edifice having been erected on the twin pillars of Wisdom and Compassion. The adept, though he must deal sternly with himself, has to cultivate kindness, sympathy, tolerance and generosity towards all sentient beings; from the very outset he performs daily meditation to develop *Bodhicitta*.

Bodhicitta (Enlightenment Mind) has two aspects; in its ultimate form it is nothing less than Wisdom itself, being the mind of the seeker now purged of delusion in union with the Universal Mind, the Buddha-Nature, Sunyata! In its relative aspect it is the mind of one so bent on Enlightenment that there is no limit to his compassion. Possessing *Bodhicitta* even in its crudest least-developed form means experiencing such *spontaneous* compassion that all beings alike are treated with the loving consideration accorded by affectionate sons and daughters to their mother. Where prejudice, aversion, selfishness or intolerance are present to the smallest degree, it is certain that *Bodhicitta* has not yet been developed. This is no matter of *striving* to love one's neighbour, but of *spontaneous* affection resulting from a stupendous revolution of the adept's mind. Compassion is held to be the essential means for Wisdom's attainment, because every thought running in a contrary direction strengthens the delusion of an 'I' in contradistinction to 'others'. In ancient times, the Chinese philosopher Mo-tzû who preached universal love was derided for prescribing an impossible ideal. Of course, impossible! No one can successfully *will* himself to love all beings without distinction; there has to be such a total shattering of the ego that distinction-free compassion dawns unimpeded of itself – though, naturally, the *wish* for such compassion must be there in the first place. Therefore the first step along the tantric path is to fix the mind on the attainment of *Bodhicitta*, to long for it above all other gifts, and thenceforth to act as far as possible as though *Bodhicitta* were already won.

Among the skilful means (*upaya*) used in tantric practice are mantras (sacred sounds); mudras (gestures); the yogas for manipulating breath, 'veins' (the body's psychic channels) and vital energy; and also mandalas (diagrams such as those which C. G. Jung recognised as being drawn from what he termed the collective unconscious).

As to mantras, it is difficult to say how they work – but, when skilfully employed, they *do* work. Explaining their power in terms of vibrations, for example, leads nowhere, for their effect has little to do with the realm of physics. Mantras, whether consisting of a single syllable or many – one contains a hundred and three syllables and there are a few much longer ones – yield no meaning to the intelligence, even in cases where at least some verbal sense can be derived. Yet they are never arbitarily invented groups of sounds; to make one up would serve no purpose. On the other hand, it is doubtful whether very exact enunciation is as important as people often suppose; for example, the parent of all mantras is pronounced AUM in Sanskrit, UM by Tibetans, ANG by Chinese and ONG by Japanese Shingon adherents, without apparent loss of effect. Perhaps rhythm and pitch are important; in any case, one is taught to intone them exactly in the manner of the teacher who transmits them. Therefore, while I pronounce most of those I use in the Tibetan manner, I retain the Japanese Shingon pronunciation of one or two learnt long ago from a Chinese disciple of a Shingon Master residing on Mount Koya in Japan. Were I to do otherwise, I am not sure they would be effective.

My failure to explain the working of mantras may seem disappointing; but then, people often employ tantric methods with as little concern for *how* they work as users of electric lamps or stoves have for the workings of electricity; what matters supremely is that they are effective. Whys and wherefores arise only when one sets out to explain them; it is humbling to discover how little *can* be explained about matters calling not for understanding at the conceptual level but direct experience. That mantric power was once more widely acknowledged than it is today is evident from many vestiges of the widespread use of mantras. Why in Christian rites is the word 'amen' left untranslated into the language being used, unless it is (or was) held to convey something lying beyond its verbal meaning? In the context of mantras, the opening passage of St John's gospel is striking – 'In the beginning was the Word.' The knowledge that 'Word' is an English rendering of 'Logos' does not take us much further; the enquiry becomes fruitful when one ponders as to why the most mystically advanced among the four gospellers should have taken 'Word' to be the fountainhead of all creation!

Closely connected with the mantric principle is the music that accompanies tantric rites. Very different from music in the commonly accepted sense, it comprises awe-inspiring sounds reminiscent of nature's wildest manifestations – the rumble of thunder, the moaning of the wind in high mountain caverns, the boom of snow-fed torrents hurtling down through precipitous chasms. The thunderous notes of the gigantic *radang*-horns, the piercing wail of thigh-bone trumpets, the sonorous thud and rattle of drums, and the clang of giant cymbals, all intermingled with the extraordinarily deep 'belly-chanting' of the lamas, echoed daily among the peaks and valleys of Mount Wu T'ai. Their solemn harmony vividly brought to mind the immensity of the great Void wherein an infinity of universes spin their way from creation to extinction, thus conjuring forth an overwhelming sense of the urgency of seeking liberation NOW – before the rare opportunity gives way to aeon-long wanderings in realms unpenetrated by the 'Lion's Roar' (the voice of Dharma). To the lamas, the ritual chants and music were all imbued by the resonance of the source and apogee of all sounds – the sacred mantra AUM.

Still less susceptible to logical explanation is the science of mudras, the gestures of power that form an inseparable part of tantric rites. Yet, here again, their efficacy was once more widely recognised than is the case today, as exemplified by the gesture used by Christian priests in bestowing benediction and the well-nigh universal placing of the hands together in prayer. The iconographic depiction of mudras to identify the Buddhas and divinities portrayed is merely subsidiary. The tantric adept, seeking to merge his three endowments of body, speech and mind with what are known as 'Body, Speech and Mind' (constituting three attributes of the supreme Wisdom-Energy) employs mudras, mantras and visualisation respectively. That mudras help in the attainment of the desired states of consciousness may perhaps be explained as being due to a subjective process of suggestion – not so the other physical component of tantric practice, the yogic manipulation of breath, 'veins' and vital essence, for this produces effects of which some at least are visible and measurable. These yogic practices would be more open than mantras or mudras to scientific investigation, were it not that the manuals setting forth both physical and mental yogas are couched in a language to which the needed key is supplied only during oral transmission from teacher to disciple, the reason being that many of them could not safely be attempted without expert guidance.

To arouse the pupil's intuitive (as opposed to merely intellectual) understanding of the theoretical basis of tantric yoga and meditation, it is usual to use some form of mandala – an arrangement of concentric squares and circles, often of great complexity and elaboration, every detail of which is pregnant with meaning. Almost all mandalas, though varied in form and complexity, are held to picture the vast macrocosm and its microcosmic counterpart, the adept's body. Most have in common an arrangement that suggests a progressive multiplication and specialisation of energies (symbolised by tiny figures of meditation Buddhas and other such figures or by single syllables or letters) as one moves outward from the centre, and a progressive unity as one moves towards it. This arrangement assists the devotee to comprehend the identity of the multiplicity of forms with the undifferentiated Source. Conversely, one may proceed from the centre, marking the successive stages of differentiation that lead ultimately to an infinite diversity. From the tiny central circle, symbolising the pure, undifferentiated Wisdom-Energy of the Void, also known as the One Mind, emanate four streams of more specialised Wisdom-Energy. These divide and sub-divide as increasing differentiation takes place towards the mandala's rim. Since this pattern is held to be universal, the mandala can be taken to symbolise a number of different, though identical, processes, of which two very important ones are: the progression from void to form that links the two aspects of reality, and the progression from the Source to the individual of the Buddha-Wisdom-Energy.

A mandala, properly expounded by a realised teacher, does help in arousing an intuitive grasp of mystical truths that become distorted when subjected to conceptualisation, as has unavoidably happened here. (Its efficacy in inspiring intuitive realisation is to some extent borne out by C. G. Jung's writings on the subject.) As students of Ch'an (Zen) know well, verbal explanations of the truths hinted at always lead to distortion or to a dead end; hence the maddening paradoxes employed by Zen Masters to shock the mind into sudden intuition.

As a support for meditation, one type of mandala is used somewhat as follows: the central point, often personified by the form of Vairocana Buddha, is viewed as supreme Wisdom streaming forth from the undifferentiated Void. The four streams of more specialised Wisdom into which it divides are each symbolised by an appropriate Buddha-form; the four become eight, personified by eight Bodhisattva-forms and the process continues to infinity, each stage and each sub-stream of differentiation being marked by a symbolic form about the significance of which the adept has been previously instructed. Now, although the Bodhisattvas and subsidiary figures standing further away from the centre are, in an absolute sense, void – as is the case with all other phenomena – at the level of relative truth whereon phenomena have a transitory existence, they represent immensely powerful forces, of which examples are

Wisdom, Compassion, Adamantine Energy, Perfect Activity and so forth. During his meditation the initiate seeks mystical union with one of these forces and thus, in a very special sense, comes to draw upon the power represented. Should he successfully identify himself with Avalokitesvara (Compassion), he will be able, to the extent that he has purified his mind of karmic hindrances, to draw upon that inexhaustible source of Compassion-Energy with the result that his thoughts while the union persists will have actual power to alleviate suffering; it will be as though a lighting system working on power generated by a small dynamo has been temporarily connected up with the main source of power.

This identification of the adept with such a being can be carried still further. Emerging from meditation, he need not separate himself, but maintain the mystical union by visualising the sacred being as abiding in his heart. This tantric counterpart of the belief 'I am God' does not, as has recently happened in some tragic cases in the West, give birth to an arrogant desire to impose his will on others or to murder and rape with the moral impunity attributed to a divine being above the law. On the contrary, it leads to a blissful freedom from self-centred thought and action, to a state of selflessness rarely attainable by other means. Such a practice, even supposing that nothing more than the adept's own subjective power is really involved (a sceptical but understandable view), must at the very least have admirable results both for the adept himself and for the beings who benefit from his compassion.

Ch'an (Zen) also pertains to the Short Path. To some followers of that system, tantric methods appear complicated and cumbersome. At a time when I still shared that view, I expressed it to one of my Tibetan teachers. His reply was more or less thus:

'The Compassionate Buddha, recognising that his teaching must be suited to people of varying attainments and propensities, himself made use of skilful means when preaching to those at different levels of understanding. You speak of the Chinese Ch'an sect as though its practice differed essentially from our own. But, within the Vajrayana, we also have methods that require no external supports, being mentally performed from first to last. If you can do without supports, well and good. You should concentrate on the Mahamudra practice, which can be performed sitting silently in a solitary place without so much as a likeness of the Blessed One to distract you. Do you really feel ready to tread that high path unaided?'

Of course, that is the point. Many people esteem Zen for its apparent simplicity, but its *successful* practice is rarer than is commonly supposed. Speaking just for myself, I have discovered that my aptitude for Zen practice is poor. On the other hand, I know people who have no affinity with tantric methods. Clearly the two 'Short Paths' are complementary, being suited to different kinds of temperament.

The Vajrayana is as richly and variously colourful as Mount Wu T'ai itself. Starting with a firm aspiration to attain *Bodhicitta*, it progresses by several routes suited to the varying capabilities of its adepts. At a certain point, set practices are left behind and the formerly binding rules no longer apply; the adept's passions and desires have been transcended. Henceforth he can enter at will that blissful state of union with the Source wherein he perceives that the whole universe revolves, as it were, within the confines of his skull – the big perfectly contained within the small exactly as expounded in the Hua Yen Sutra.

For adepts not gifted with the iron resolution needed to reach the goal in this very life, the aim is to attain a sufficient diminution of evil karmic propensities to ensure rebirth in an environment propitious to continuation of the quest. Those who aim no higher than very modest progress do not need to resort to tantric means to follow successfully their less arduous path; but some choose to employ the meditation methods pertaining to the lower tantras which involve neither physical yogas nor especially arduous training. What must not ever be discarded is the aspiration to generate *Bodhicitta* and for this it is necessary to cultivate a broadly tantric attitude of mind, which involves: determination to use all circumstances that come one's way as means contributing to spiritual progress, applying the doctrine of voidness as a remedy for the persistent hindrances caused by the ego, recognising mind as the only reality, and living in accordance with the tantric injunction to *see all beings as Buddhas, hear all sounds as mantra and perceive all places to be Nirvana*. (How this injunction can be employed at the level of daily life will be set forth in the concluding chapter.)

The effectiveness of such exotic aids to progress as mantras, mudras, mandalas and so forth is readily apparent only to certain kinds of people – those who have discovered it by practice, those born within an ambience where such methods are taken for granted; and certain others who have the ability to recognise individuals far advanced towards realisation. In this third category are those Westerners who, perceiving the wisdom and spirituality of the lamas under whom they study, are prepared to accept the efficacy of the tantric methods which form an essential part of the lamas' own methods of cultivation. No faith in miracles is involved here; it is like taking it for granted that a highly skilled physician owes a great deal to the excellence of his training and experience, first as a medical student and later during the course of his practice. Nevertheless, the employment of mantras and mudras is so foreign to our experience that most of us are bound to feel doubt, if not to make the mistake of regarding them as mumbo-jumbo. Many feel they would be convinced if only they had an opportunity to behold a display of extraordinary powers attained by tantric means. Unfortunately that is seldom easy to arrange; one stumbles upon such convincing evidence by chance or, more often, not at all. Tantric yogins, regarding the paranormal powers that arise in them as being more of a hindrance than help to progress, shun such displays, except in very rare circumstances. They are a hindrance for two reasons: in the

K

first place such powers can very easily become a source of false pride, exciting as they do the admiration (and sometimes envy) of the uninitiated; in the second, they tend to attract followers, but not for the right reason; for one who studies tantra in the hope of gaining paranormal powers sinks deeper into delusion, thus wasting his own and his lama's precious time. As it happens, though, there is just one such power that soon becomes evident to those who have much to do with advanced adepts – that of telepathy which, besides developing quickly and rather easily as an elementary by-product of tantric practice, is as hard to conceal as the ability to see, or hear or read.

As it would be disappointing to give no examples at all of phenomena that would verify the effectiveness of tantric methods even in the eyes of people not convinced of the validity of mystical experience, I shall now digress to describe one particular yogic effect which, though very ordinary by tantric standards, is probably inexplicable in terms of medical science and yet can be made to occur after just a few days of by no means arduous practice. Though superficially comparable to the phenomenon of stigmata, it cannot be medically explained in the same way, since no building up of tense emotion is involved. Therefore, if the veracity of myself and my informant can, as I hope, be taken for granted, it may seem in its way quite striking. The story concerns an Englishwoman and two Canadians who practised a yoga known as *powa*. It is a secret yoga, but as several accounts of it have been published in English, there would seem to be no harm in setting forth the general idea as a prelude to my anecdote. Briefly, the purpose of *powa* is to ensure that, at the moment of death, the consciousness will leave the body by a special aperture in the crown of the head and enter a Buddha-form visualised as being seated just above the crown, instead of departing through the usual orifices. This feat, coupled with a certain visualisation performed by the dying man and the preparations he has made in advance, will prevent his falling into one of the more unfortunate (because spiritually sterile) modes of rebirth. Like most yogas, whether of Chinese or Indian origin, *powa* intimately concerns the central 'vein' (psychic channel) running from near the base of the spine to a point very close to the crown of the head. The practice consists essentially of visualising the form of Amitayus Buddha immediately above one's head and mentally creating a small object within one's own body which, by the power of consciousness, is driven upwards along the central 'vein' and, with the help of the mantric seed-syllable HRIK, forced to the crown where, when the practice has been properly performed over a certain period, a tiny aperture opens of itself ready for use at the moment of death. *Powa*, however, is dangerous and will shorten the adept's life unless remedial steps are taken.

To begin my story. During my teenage days in England, I read in one of Madame David-Neil's books an account of Tibetan *powa* adepts who, on successfully concluding a brief period of training, would present themselves before their lama, each with a long stalk of *kusa*-grass planted upright in the newly opened aperture. Not surprisingly, I told myself that the apertures must have been fraudulently made with a nail or sharp instrument, probably to win a little fame for the lama and disciples concerned. However, several years later while living in China, I read a newspaper account of a great rite held in a temple somewhere in central China (I think it was Nanking), at which a few dozen Chinese disciples who had been studying under a visiting Mongol lama appeared in public with stalks of *kusa*-grass implanted in 'magically opened' apertures in their skulls to indicate their mastery of *powa*. By that time I knew enough to be certain that tantric methods are capable of producing physical effects a great deal more remarkable than that; even so, I had some doubts because it appeared that the Chinese disciples had none of them undergone the long periods of solitude and the austerities that form part of most kinds of yogic training within the Vajrayana system. Still, the event aroused my interest and remained in my memory.

A few weeks ago, a very good friend of mine came to stay with

K*

me – an Englishwoman of about thirty years of age who has spent the last ten years as a Tibetan nun and was on her way to Hong Kong to receive the Chinese Bhiksuni ordination. A person of lively intelligence, modest about her own attainments and inclined generally to minimise such marvels as she has encountered during her long sojourn among Tibetan yogins, she is the last person in the world to tell tall stories or sacrifice truth for the purpose of producing an effect. It was in passing and without any consciousness of saying anything especially remarkable that she related the following account of *powa* practice. We shall call her Ani-la, a polite Tibetan title for nuns.

Ani-la's mother, while on a visit to her daughter in one of those Tibetan settlements that nestle in the Indian foot-hills of the Himalayas, was persuaded to practise *powa*. Ani-la herself, being on a different path, was not permitted to join her in the practice, but had to be present to interpret each time the old lady went to their lama for instruction. All the mother had to do was to perform the *powa* yogic visualisation for about an hour each morning and evening. However, after a few days, she decided not to go forward with it, being alarmed by the onset of strange physical sensations in the top of her head; moreover, Ani-la was becoming anxious on her own account because, merely reflecting upon the lama's instructions while interpreting his discourse to her mother caused her similarly unpleasant sensations of icy cold alternating with heat, severe itching and sometimes actual pain at the top of the skull – and, once or twice, another lama present had had to rouse her suddenly by a sharp reminder that she was there to interpret, not to take part in the *powa* practice. It seems that the lama-instructor was himself ejaculating the mantric HRIK at appropriate moments and that the syllable, imbued with his own power, was producing this strange and rapid effect.

Shortly after the old lady retired from the practice, two Canadian women took it up under the same lama and, within as little as four or five days, the expected tiny apertures opened at the crown, exuding a small quantity of blood and lymph. Even though such quick success may have been attributable to the mind force of their instructor, Ani-la assured me that a week or two is normally sufficient to produce the same effect in most people.

In the vast context of Vajrayana practice, this story is perhaps too trivial to warrant the space expended on it, but it does offer a convincing illustration of the power of mind acting upon matter – which, in a sense, is what the whole of Mahayana Buddhism is about. If mind and matter were distinct from each other, as our learned scientists supposed until not very long ago, then mystical aspiration and practice throughout the world, from the beginning of history until now, could be dismissed as moonshine and the venerable mystical traditions of East and West accounted worthless as an idiot's dream. On the other hand, when mind is recognised as an emanation of Mind and matter as nothing more or less than Mind's reflection, then one sees how wonderful, how precious are the secrets handed down by those deeply experienced in the realisation of mystical union between mind and Mind!

Such secrets cannot be plumbed by talk – they must be lived! No descriptions, though they be of marvels ten thousand times more wonderful than the one described above, no demonstrations of paranormal powers, no coming face to face with beings far advanced along the path can do more than hint at what lies beyond appearances. To convince a sceptic of the illusory nature of matter would be as hard a task as convincing an ancient Viking voyager that the world is round; these two facts are equally at variance with the direct evidence of the senses which, though they function in the darkness of primordial delusion, are so often taken for the ultimate touchstone of truth. It does no good to argue. Understanding must proceed from the innermost chamber of the mind.

The promptings of intuition are unfailingly there for those who seek them, but its voice can be heard only amidst stillness. Stillness of mind, not always silence. Indeed there are sounds that are powerfully conducive to the sudden transposition of consciousness from a state of blindness to one of soft, inner brilliance – the music of the waves, the song of a cicada, the thunder of a mountain torrent, the howling of a gale sweeping through a mountain pass, the resonant UUUUUUUUUUUU-UUUUUUUUUUUUM of the lamas' *radangs*, the crash of drums and clang of cymbals, the tinkle of silver or jade, these and a thousand other sounds produced by the elements or by the rhythmic striking of natural substances such as metal, wood or stone. There are sights and odours, too, imbued with this same power; but most conducive of all is a state of mind – the shining objectless awareness known as the seeing with nought seen and the hearing with nought heard. It is this inner perception that is most precious, for what is perceived from without is so distorted by the disordered senses that its is-ness is often lost; whereas, from the innermost recesses of the mind, light streams forth without hindrance.

All the paths, both long and short, ever devised for the attainment of mystical perception – self-realisation, blissful union – are but variations of the path that, going from nowhere to nowhere, begins and ends *within*! That the Vajrayana offers highly effective means for pursuing this path may be judged from the qualities of its gifted adherents – their deep spirituality, sincerity, warmth of heart and their tranquil gaiety in the face of dire adversity. Those who have been misled by travellers tales, or (as I was), by the startling nature of tantric symbols, into supposing that the Vajrayana is a decadent form of spiritual endeavour, have only to encounter a few of its accomplished exponents to be convinced of the exalted nature of its doctrine and practice.

Chapter 8

Remedies for Discontent?

From the response aroused in the West by Ch'an (Zen) and, more recently, tantric Buddhism, it seems possible that Eastern mystical traditions uprooted from their native soil are destined to flower anew beyond the seas. Circumstances may not be propitious for them to flourish vigorously; many of the seedlings may soon die, but here and there the roots may take firm hold and adapt themselves well to the new soil. Much will depend on whether the first generation to receive the transmission (from such sources as the handful of Chinese monks now teaching in the United States or the communities of Tibetan lamas established in the Himalayan foot-hills) succeed in taking more than just the shadow of what is offered, and on whether they attract followers of sufficient calibre for the new-founded lines to continue. For it is inherent in the nature of mystical traditions that they cannot be learnt from books. Precious though the sacred texts may be, the life of such traditions resides in oral teaching that can be imparted only by men far advanced along the path to self-realisation.

A few decades ago, even qualified optimism would have seemed misplaced. The Western mind, after close on two thousand years of being dominated by the image of a father-God, had come to substitute an impersonal, utopian image whose glitter has already tarnished. Capitalists and communists alike were convinced that the way to universal happiness and prosperity lay in looking forward and *outward*, that science had brought us to the brink of creating a bounteous society able to fulfil all social and material needs and thus ensure contentment. Today their dreams lie shattered. The plundering of nature's wealth for man's enrichment is bringing dire disaster to the environment; the tragic gap between 'have' and 'have-not' peoples grows ever wider; and the spectre of war hovers always close at hand. Most unlooked-for of all has been the discovery that, even in affluent nations whose citizens enjoy large measures of welfare and security, happiness remains elusive! In these disturbing circumstances, people are beginning to recognise the barrenness of the materialist approach to happiness and enquiring spirits have begun to examine the mystic's aphorism 'Look *within*!'

Not long ago my twenty-five-year-old son voiced an urgent longing to 'break away from it all'. Asked whether he were unhappy, he replied: 'Happiness? For my generation the pay's alright. It covers food, clothes and rent, leaving enough over for running an old car and occasionally whooping things up. But mostly we work at depressingly routine jobs, go home to supper, watch TV a bit or maybe pop out for a drink with friends, then tumble into bed and that's about all. Growing older brings no real change besides more pay and more responsibilities. True, there are no hardships in this sort of life, no struggle for survival – but is slaving to timetables and machines the good life we hoped for as kids? Is that all there is?'

Well, mysticism offers no broad remedies for modern ills. Poverty of the tragic kind found, say, in India or Bangladesh demands vast-scale collective action and so does the terrifyingly rapid deterioration of the environment; but boredom and discontent in the midst of plenty are a problem for the individual and it is here that the ancient mystical traditions may be looked to for an answer. Only, before going further, I should like to stress two points: first, that I am innocent of missionary intention and do not for one moment advocate wholesale conversion to traditions that are still largely alien to the West; second, that what remedies occur to me are strictly for a certain kind of individual, being so intensely personal that whoever accepts them is obliged to do something drastic for himself that neither God nor man can do on his behalf.

The First Step

To enquirers like my son, I would say: 'Remember that mind
is the king. Of mind is frustration born; by mind is life endowed
with happiness and meaning.' Since not many such enquirers
are likely to be potential mystics, I would begin by suggesting
cultivation of a mental attitude that could, not too fancifully,
be called Taoistic; this much could be achieved without the
austerities demanded of Short Path adepts whose thirst for
the bliss that arises from within makes them ready for great
sacrifices. Indeed, the achievement could be almost effortless,
being carried out in the spirit of *wu-wei*.

Forced slavery is rare these days; rather, servitude is willingly
embraced by those eager for wealth and status, though the
eagerness may arise less from greed than from the assumption
that what most people seem to want so much must be supremely
worth having. For the sake of wealth, people already well
above the poverty line slave all their lives, not realising that
withdrawal from the rat-race would immediately increase
rather than diminish their wealth. Obviously anyone who
finds the full satisfaction of all his material desires well within
his means can be said to be wealthy; it follows that, except by
the truly poor, wealth can be achieved overnight by a change of
mental attitude that will set bounds to desires. As Laotzû put
it, 'He who is contented always has enough.' This is a principle
completely lost sight of by present-day society. Like helpless
birds mesmerised by serpents, we allow self-appointed arbiters
of fashion to dictate length of skirt and width of trousers, thus
gulling us into unnecessarily replenishing our wardrobes every
year, instead of being satisfied with what is comfortable and
pleasing to ourselves. This is slavery indeed – voluntary slavery
to manufacturers and advertisers whose cynical purpose is to
seduce us into buying what is entirely unnecessary to our well-
being. For those unfortunates who suffer actual want, a very
different remedy is needed; as to the rest, the act of withdrawing
the mind from the race for wealth and status and making
freedom to be oneself the goal would enrich them at one bound –

mentally, spiritually and, in an important sense, materially. All the energy and time expended on keeping up with the Changs and the Joneses would be freed for constructive use. Incidentally, status, the second object of the rat-race, is an even more illusory benefit than wealth, the pleasure it confers being purely relative; however high one climbs, there are always others higher – and, as Laotzû said: 'He who stands on tiptoe, totters.' On the other hand, caring nothing for prestige and public opinion confers a relaxation that knows no bounds.

How wonderful were the ancient Taoist sages! Calling them cloud-riding immortals was not wholly a figure of speech, for the sense of freedom that comes from renouncing ambition, being true to one's own principles without the least concern about what others think and learning to accept with equanimity all that life or death may bring, is a draught so heady that those who have quaffed it feel as exultant as if sun, moon and stars were their playthings. Absolved of anxiety, they revel in a weightlessness of spirit closely comparable to the lightness of body needed for riding upon clouds.

The achievement of joyous tranquillity should prove a satisfying remedy for discontent. As to those who wish to go further, they should begin by taking this same step, for the freedom of spirit won by frugality is indispensible to success in attaining the much more difficult goal of intuitive wisdom.

The Second Step

The essence of tantric practice is that the adept learn how to harness the energy of everything whatsoever – good, bad and indifferent – to the task of self-realisation. When, almost twenty years ago, I began to study tantric Buddhism seriously, I went first to a Mongolian Geshé (highly qualified exponent of the Dharma) who began by expounding the inner meaning of the passage: 'See all beings as the Buddha! Hear all sounds as mantra! Recognise all places as Nirvana!' These are much more than pious injunctions rooted in Mahayana doctrine, for they inculcate a tantric attitude to life whereby many marvels can be wrought. It is this that I would next recommend to enquirers like my son, regardless of whether or not they are Buddhist. In part, the practice for attaining this attitude of mind may seem at the early stages like a system of make-believe; that is to say, while still at the level of relative truth and as yet unable to experience the divine perception whereby all dualism (e.g. between Buddhas and ordinary beings, between sounds pleasing and discordant, between sights beautiful and ugly) is negated, one tries to behave *as if* in the light of that perception. The purpose is to discipline the mind in such a manner as to make the experience much easier to attain. If in the fairy-tale, Beauty had known the hideous Beast for a handsome young prince temporarily transformed and had learnt to visualise him as he really was, her love would have blossomed more readily and the kiss that revealed him in his original form been given the sooner.

'See all beings as the Buddha' refers doctrinally both to the potentiality for Enlightenment (Buddhahood) with which every being is endowed (cf. the Christian term, 'the Christ within') and, what is more important in this context, to the state of absolute truth wherein exists no distinction between mind and Mind, delusion and Wisdom. In practice, revering all beings as supremely holy, no matter how gross or monstrous some may appear to be, just as one esteems the wish-fulfilling gem whether housed in an ivory casket or hidden in a dung-heap, means discarding every grain of scorn, malice, hatred, cruelty. No one sincerely dedicated to this practice would wilfully harm others, discriminate among them or withhold sympathy, compassion and whatever aid lay within his power. Of course attaining such an attitude is easier said than done –lifelong habits and preju- dices are hard to set aside – but the very aspiration to see all beings as holy makes one kinder and more tolerant. Carrying the practice further revolutionises one's character; ugly and perverse qualities decrease by leaps and bounds.

'Hear all sounds as mantra,' that is to say as holy, also relates to the doctrine that phenomena in their absolute state are beyond duality, from which it follows that 'raucous' and 'melodious' are illusory distinctions. The practice is comparatively easy; one learns to hear 'raucous' as 'melodious' by a process similar to playing the children's game of seeing pictures in the fire. Soon one can mentally convert the din of midnight traffic into something just as noisy but pleasant, such as the roar of ocean waves dashing against a rocky shore. The immediate consequence is to eliminate what, for city-dwellers especially, constitutes one of the greatest sources of disturbance in modern life. The further consequence and true purpose is to win increasing perception of the holiness inherent in all things.

'Recognise all places as Nirvana' is an injunction to perceive things as they really are. Since the myriad transient forms comprise an aspect of the undifferentiated Void, there can be no *leaving* the realm of form, no *entering* Nirvana, but simply a cleansing of the mind that results in direct perception of what has always been from the first. 'Going to' resolves itself into awakening to 'what is here'. In practice, this task is the easiest of the three, being (at the earliest stage) analogous to conjuring delightful figures from the patterns formed by frost on glass or the grain of a flat wooden surface, or willing one's eyes to discern glimpses of sea amidst a vista of blue hills, or viewing clouds as peaks and peaks as clouds. Presently one comes to see beauty in the most unpromising surroundings – bleak concrete yards or grimy brick walls. Dung takes on the loveliness of amber; spittle is recognised as partaking of the holy essence of the Void. It is not a matter of learning to perceive falsely, but of teaching mind and senses to recognise the beauty and holiness of all that is. Once, when driving, I came upon what seemed to be a mass of lovely scarlet blossom clothing distant trees, only to find on drawing nearer some ordinary trees fenced by corrugated zinc with a coating of red lead. What I had seen as exquisitely beautiful now struck me as intensely ugly, yet nothing in the scene had changed, only the manner of my viewing. The experience brought home to me that beauty and ugliness are but the creations of our own minds.

Acquiring a tantric attitude, though still far removed from

the attainment of intuitive wisdom, creates a lively awareness of the perfection transfusing the world of form. Were someone like my son to get thus far, he might be content to rest in that joyful state, but it is likely he would need no urging to go further. Those who sense imminent reality envision it sometimes as a divine being, sometimes as a divine state. What matters is not whether one thinks of it as God of Tao, but the certainty of its existence. This certainty is what in Mahayana terminology is called 'faith'; but faith in an ultimate perfection not conceptually defined differs greatly from faith centred upon a particular concept and name, whether Allah or Jehova, and no other. Buddhists are discouraged from attempting to conceptualise what is intuitively apprehended; to all attempts to define it, the Buddhist answer is 'Not so, not so, not so.' Similarly Taoists hold that whatever can be conveyed in words is not the Eternal Tao.

The Third Step
For those who desire to go still further, acquiring such an attitude of mind must be accompanied by contemplative practice. The sense of something infinitely holy transfusing all that is perceived arouses a thirst for clear, direct perception of that sublime reality. To attain it, ego-consciousness must be progressively purged; wherever a sense of 'I' and 'IT' ('HIM') and of 'I' and 'others' persists, duality – that king of demons – continues to deceive. The finite mind must address itself to realising its unity with Mind. This is a hard task, for the seeming 'ego', albeit no more than the illusory creation of dualistic thought, is powerful enough to fight tenaciously for continued recognition as 'the real me'. To frugal living and the containment of inordinate desires must now be added firm discipline. It is a dangerous error to suppose that, at this stage, the adept is ready to discard all rules of conduct on the grounds that good and evil, being a dual concept, cannot in reality exist, or that passion must be given free rein to destroy passion; though both these doctrines are valid, they pertain to the

realm of absolute truth and are suited only to adepts who, having successfully practised rigorous austerity for many years, have transcended the stage of responding to ego-prompted desire; were people of less than great attainment to renounce self-discipline, contemplative practice would be attended by certain failure. The stress placed by Buddhist meditation teachers on the need for restraint may discourage beginners, who are likely to react to it by exclaiming: 'What you preach is positively calvinistic in its joylessness!' But that is a confused and superficial view. Enjoyment that causes no hurt is not held to be sinful; when adepts on the Short Path renounce certain pleasures, the restrictions are analogous to those governing an athlete's training; those who undertake a valorous task voluntarily accept a mode of life not required of ordinary people; moreover, the joys they renounce are as nothing compared with those they expect to attain.

Just as intensive meditation unaccompanied by a special discipline would surely prove a waste of effort, so, too, it would be folly to practise it without simultaneously cultivating compassion – the surest antidote to discrimination between 'self' and 'other'. Such qualities as frugality, restraint and overflowing compassion are contrary to what is often said to be human nature, but they are fully consonant with one's *real* nature which, as the meditator presently discovers, is not 'his' at all. As to the method of meditation and whether certain physical yogas should accompany it, or whether some other method such as concentration upon a sacred formula should replace it – these depend on individual aptitudes. For some, an overtly devotional approach is best; for some, the Ch'an (Zen) methods; for others, a more nearly intellectual approach like that of the Pure Consciousness Sect. Only an able meditation teacher familiar with his pupil's character and capabilities is in a position to give advice on this matter. In all cases, to attain that direct perception of reality which is the crown of mystical experience requires an unswerving dedication that makes great demands upon the adept.

I have observed that Westerners generally are prone to a danger that scarcely arises among Asians. Whether because of over-dependence upon intellect or because they fight shy of attitudes reminiscent of the religion of their childhood, they tend to disdain devotional practices. Nevertheless, a profound sense of reverence, awe, devotion is essential. Though it is from Ch'an (Zen) texts that a concept of non-devotional Buddhism derives, I doubt if there are Ch'an (Zen) temples anywhere in the East where offerings are not made before statues of the Buddhas and of the Wisdom Bodhisattva, Manjusri. No matter what provisional concept one may hold (whether of a divine being, divine state or divine state of being), reverence cannot be dispensed with; for then the meditator must surely fall into the error of reflecting '*I* have progressed thus far', '*I* have attained such and such a state' – thoughts which instantly negate all progress by giving new life to that pertinacious delusion, 'I'. For all that Ch'an (Zen) meditation stresses 'self-power', Chinese and Japanese adepts seldom question the identity of 'self-power' and 'other-power', since 'inside' and 'outside' are meaningless in connection with space-transcending mind.

I particularly treasure the advice of one of my Tibetan teachers who, speaking of levels of practice suited to varying degrees of understanding and attainment, said: 'Some start by worshipping an external object as though it were a self-existent deity; next they are taught to visualise the object of devotion as residing in their hearts, then to perceive that self and object are identical; and finally all concepts are abandoned. But, at whichever level you practise, learn to embrace them all; for each expresses an aspect of truth that it would be unwise to discard.'

Similarly, in temples of the Ch'an Sect, though meditation is of the 'self-power' kind, devotional rites are daily performed, lest the meditators lose perspective with dangerous consequences. Although it is clearly recognised that the celestial Buddhas and Bodhisattvas are personifications of various attributes of the Wisdom streaming from Pure Mind (apart from which neither they nor any other beings or objects can be said to exist), during devotional rites they are treated *as though* they were actual deities. To regard them as separate from one's own mind (which is also Mind) would be delusion, yet they cannot be dismissed like characters in an unfounded legend (Father Christmas, for example); at the level of relative truth, the entities they personify exist. The objection that worshipping celestial beings involves an element of make-believe can also be met in another way. In a universe where naught but Mind exists, all concepts, all objects are ultimately void (and therefore make-believe); what is thought or dreamed or visualised is no less real than what is objectively perceived.

In my view, when a Christian mystic deep in prayer or meditation experiences a divine response, when a Pure Land devotee feels the presence of Amitabha or Kuanyin, and when a Ch'an meditator feels Mind respond to mind, all three are visited by an identical experience; yet it might not do for them to interchange their methods, since each has been conditioned to conceive of the Inconceivable in his own way. With the dawning of intuitive wisdom in their minds, they will be able to laugh together at their former differences.

The reason why 'other-power' methods are more effective in some cases appears to me simple, though it may not be simple to convey. With the 'self-power' method taught in Ch'an monasteries, a degree of effort is involved. Well, in a sense, all meditation involves effort in that one pursues a certain course in order to achieve a goal; but, in another sense, it must be effortless; there must be no straining of the mind. When engaged in 'other-power' meditation, it is easier to dispense with effort. The adept says to himself: 'Stop striving! There is nothing you can do of yourself. Just be still and attentive.' With stillness, something, as it were, 'enters in', but not until, besides abandoning effort, one has abandoned also the desire for attainment; for such desire (or its converse, fear of failure) creates a stir that mars mind's perfect stillness. If I have not made my point, I am sorry I have no better way of expressing it. One thing is sure: what is apprehended by some as a particular and exclusive being (God), by others as a celestial 'being' of their own or their teacher's choosing, and by yet others as no being at all is in all three cases identical.

Where the mystic's path is concerned, I doubt that any real importance attaches to whether the adept subscribes to one religion or another (although Buddhism and Taoism do have the advantage that, besides *openly* proclaiming the supremacy of mystical experience, they have evolved very effective methods of attaining it). I hope that this rather personal account of some aspects of Chinese and Tibetan mysticism will be of interest to people of many faiths; for it should not be difficult to adapt contemplative methods to any sort of doctrine – the more so as, beyond a certain point, doctrinal differences cease to matter one iota.

Though the Way is arduous and those who follow it are some-times beset by fiends – boredom, frustration, sensuous longing, discouragement, despair – the goal is unutterably sublime. One glimpse of its splendour is enough to rout those fiends for long enough to gain new courage to defy them. Of the many names given to the Nameless, I love best the Taoist term, Tao or Way, just because it has no flavour of a special creed or concept. May there be followers of the Way for as long as the universe endures and may they be happy in the knowledge that they belong to a band of men whose compassion has leavened with sweetness this strife-torn earth since the beginning of recorded history!

Short Glossary

Only those foreign terms whose meaning may not be clear from the context each time they appear are given below:

Bodhicitta	'Enlightenment Mind', a mind characterised by supreme Wisdom and Compassion.
Bodhisattva(s)	1. Beings approaching Buddahood; 2. personifications or embodiments of transcendent qualities.
Buddha(s)	1. Beings who attained Enlightenment from the human state; 2. embodiments of various aspects of Wisdom-Compassion Energy, regarded by some as actual beings, by others as symbolising the qualities they personify.
Ch'an	Called Zen in Japan, the name of a sect and also of a method of attaining self-realisation; it emphasises 'self-power' as opposed to 'other-power'.
Dakini	Tantric consort.
Dharani	A mantra or sacred formula in written form.
Dharma	The Doctrine of the Buddha, also Universal Law.
dharma(s)	Transient units of existence, tiny bursts of energy; also, every kind of phenomenon.
hua-t'ou	A conundrum to be solved intuitively, called 'koan' in Japan.
kaoliang	Grain coarser than maize.
Kargyupa	A Tibetan sect notable for meditation and austerity.
karma	The chain of cause and effect, activity set in train by thought, word and deed, leading to rebirth.
koan	See hua-t'ou.
kung-an	Very similar to hua-t'ou or koan (q.v.).
lama	1. In common parlance, a Tibetan-style monk. 2. Properly speaking, a Tibetan term for a monk *or layman* learned in the Buddhist religion.

Mahayana The school of Buddhism prevalent in all Buddhist countries except those of southeast Asia; its doctrines are derived from the Sanskrit version of the Buddhist Canon.

mantra A word of power, a sacred formula.

mudra A gesture of power, a sacred gesture.

Nirvana The final state achieved by beings after Enlightenment. Beyond description, it cannot be said either to exist or not exist in the ordinary sense of those terms, but it is held to be a state of bliss.

radang An immensely long Tibetan horn.

samadhi A one-pointed state of consciousness free from sensory perception.

samsara Opposite of Nirvana, the universe as perceived by ordinary unrealised beings, a state inherently unsatisfactory.

Shakyamuni Buddha The Founder of Buddhism, Gautama Buddha.

Sunyata The Great Void, a term for Ultimate Reality.

tantra A system of spiritual cultivation utilising all circumstances whatsoever to achieve self-realisation.

Tao The Way, a Chinese term for Ultimate Reality as the mother, container and true 'substance' of the universe.

Tathagata(s) The Thus-Come, a title of the Buddha(s).

Theravada Also known as Hinayana, the school of Buddhism prevalent in southeast Asia. Its Canon is in the Pali tongue.

vajra An adamantine substance or object symbolising the indestructibility of the Dharma.

Vajrayana The tantric school of Buddhism prevalent in Mongolia and Tibet.

wu-wei A Taoist term literally meaning 'no activity', but actually meaning no activity that is not spontaneous and free from calculation.

yinyang A Chinese symbol representing the negative and positive (female and male) aspects of all phenomena.

Zen The Japanese term for Ch'an (q.v.).